Talk About Teaching!

Second Edition

Talk About Teaching!

Leading Professional Conversations

Second Edition

Charlotte Danielson

CORWIN
A SAGE Company

FOR INFORMATION:

Corwin

A SAGE Company

2455 Teller Road

Thousand Oaks, California 91320

(800) 233-9936

www.corwin.com

SAGE Publications Ltd.

1 Oliver's Yard

55 City Road

London EC1Y 1SP

United Kingdom

SAGE Publications India Pvt. Ltd.

B 1/I 1 Mohan Cooperative Industrial Area

Mathura Road, New Delhi 110 044

India

SAGE Publications Asia-Pacific Pte. Ltd.

3 Church Street

#10-04 Samsung Hub

Singapore 049483

Executive Editor: Arnis Burvikovs

Senior Associate

  Editor: Desirée A. Bartlett

Editorial Assistant: Andrew Olson

Production Editor: Amy Joy Schroller

Copy Editor: Diane DiMura

Typesetter: C&M Digitals (P) Ltd.

Proofreader: Laura Webb

Indexer: Karen Wiley

Cover Designer: Anupama Krishnan

Marketing Manager: Amy Vader

Printed in the United States of America

ISBN 978-1-4833-7379-9

This book is printed on acid-free paper.

SUSTAINABLE FORESTRY INITIATIVE

Certified Chain of Custody

Promoting Sustainable Forestry

www.sfiprogram.org

SFI-01268

SFI label applies to text stock

15 16 17 18 19 10 9 8 7 6 5 4 3 2 1

Contents

Preface to the Second Edition

In the six years since the first edition of *Talk About Teaching* was published, the educational landscape has changed considerably. Schools—and increasingly individual teachers—are being held to high standards of accountability for student learning. How that student growth is measured is still subject to ongoing debate: What constitutes evidence of student learning, and how is it attributed to individual teachers? But it would appear that incorporating measure of student growth, of some sort, will be a permanent fixture of systems of teacher evaluation moving forward.

But to the extent that the quality of teaching is the most important contributor (at least of factors within the school) of student learning, the imperative to improve that learning translates directly into a parallel imperative to strengthen teaching practice. This, in turn, yields a need to engage in those activities known to promote teacher learning, namely, self-assessment, reflection on practice, and professional conversation.

Hence, the need to *Talk About Teaching* is more important than ever; in a high-stakes accountability environment surrounding teacher evaluation, it's essential that teachers have the opportunity, in a culture of professional inquiry, to strengthen their practice.

There is, in addition, a second reason to engage deeply in conversations around teaching practice: The demands for student learning have been increasing, in some situations dramatically. A number of states have adopted the Common Core State Standards and the accompanying assessments of student learning as official policy. Other states, while deciding against those student standards, have adopted their own rigorous standards for student learning. Whether at the national or state level, more rigorous standards for student learning demand teaching at higher levels: for conceptual understanding, advanced cognitive processes, and the skills of argumentation. For some teachers, this constitutes a "heavy lift" and demands teaching in new and more rigorous ways.

Thus, the combination of factors—more rigorous procedures for teacher evaluation, and higher standards for student learning—create a need for improved teaching practice. One of the most powerful mechanisms for the improvement of teaching is professional conversation and the skills to *Talk About Teaching*.

The second edition of *Talk About Teaching* reflects the altered landscape surrounding teacher evaluation, and the continuing imperative to enhance opportunities for teachers to strengthen their craft. In addition to an updating the references and a completely new design and graphics, the implications of higher standards for student learning (in some states as adopted Common Core State Standards) are embedded in the sections describing important student learning. Lastly, Chapter 4 ("Topics for Conversation") has been almost entirely rewritten to reflect the profession's evolving understanding of accomplished teaching.

Preface to *Talk About Teaching*

Leadership in schools implies instructional leadership. All educators who exercise either formal or informal leadership (site administrators, department chairs, team leaders, curriculum coordinators, instructional coaches, or informal teacher leaders) have the responsibility to use their influence and positional authority to ensure high levels of student learning. This sometimes involves challenging accepted wisdom; at other times, it means contributing new insights or the results of recent research findings.

Teaching is enormously complex work, and enhancing one's skill is a career-long endeavor. New discoveries about teaching and learning are made on an ongoing basis; it is an obligation of every teacher, and a mark of true professionalism, to stay abreast of developments in the subjects they teach and in the associated principles of pedagogy. Ongoing learning, in other words, is inherent to the responsibility of teaching. Supporting that learning, therefore, is an essential obligation of instructional leadership.

So what contributes to and promotes teacher learning? How can school leaders ensure a culture of professional inquiry in which such learning is accepted as an essential component of the work of teaching and in which such teacher learning is maximized? What are the mechanisms through which teacher learning occurs?

An important mechanism to promote teacher learning, in addition to the traditional approaches of professional reading and workshops, is that of conversation. Through focused and occasionally structured conversation, teachers are encouraged to think deeply about their work, to reflect on their approaches and student responses. And yet conducting such conversations requires skill. Many teachers assume that if their principal or supervisor wants to discuss the events of a classroom, it means that there is something wrong or that there is a concern. But by neglecting to engage in professional conversations with teachers, educational leaders decline to take advantage of one of the most powerful tools at their disposal to promote teacher learning.

There are three different categories of professional conversations:

- Formal reflective conversations following a formal observation conducted for the purpose of teacher evaluation

- Coaching conversations, in which the teacher invites an administrator or colleague to provide another set of eyes in providing feedback on some specific aspect of practice

- Informal professional conversations that follow a principal's brief, unannounced observations of professional practice in action in a lesson

The first two of these types of conversations, formal reflective conversations and coaching conversations, have been fully described in the professional literature. The last, informal professional conversations, deserves more exploration and may have the greatest potential to affect practice. They are the focus of this book.

Acknowledgments

In preparing the second edition of *Talk About Teaching*, I'm indebted to hundreds of educators in the United States and overseas, who have contacted me about the content of the book and its value to them in their work. In addition, the consultants in the Danielson Group have incorporated its concepts into the work they do with teachers and school leaders across the country and around the globe; I'm most grateful to them for their efforts in spreading these important ideas into their work. And lastly, Shelly Arneson, a Danielson Group consultant, offered invaluable feedback and suggestions for strengthening the second edition; I'm most appreciative to her for that.

Publisher's Acknowledgments

Corwin gratefully acknowledges the contributions of the following reviewers:

M. Susan Bolte
Principal
Providence Elementary
Aubrey, TX

Diane Canino Rispoli
Clinical Professor of Educational Leadership and former school leader
Syracuse University
Syracuse, NY

Charles L. Lowery
School Principal
Woodville ISD
Woodville, TX

About the Author

Charlotte Danielson, a former economist, is an internationally recognized expert in the area of teacher effectiveness, specializing in the design of teacher evaluation systems that, while ensuring teacher quality, also promote professional learning. She advises state education departments and national ministries and departments of education, both in the United States and overseas. She is in demand as a keynote speaker at national and international conferences and as a policy consultant to legislatures and administrative bodies.

Ms. Danielson is a graduate of Cornell University (history), Oxford University (philosophy, politics, and economics), and Rutgers University (educational administration and supervision). She has taught at all levels, kindergarten through university, and has worked as a curriculum director and staff development director, and is the founder of The Danielson Group. Her Framework for Teaching has become the most widely used definition of teaching in the United States and has been adopted as the single model, or one of several approved models, in over twenty states.

Ms. Danielson's many publications range from defining good teaching (*Enhancing Professional Practice: A Framework for Teaching* (2nd ed., 2007), to organizing schools for student success (*Enhancing Student Achievement: A Framework for School Improvement*, 2002), to teacher leadership (*Teacher Leadership That Strengthens Professional Practice*, 2006), to professional conversations (*Talk About Teaching! Conducting Professional Conversations*, 2009), to numerous practical instruments and training programs (both onsite and online) to assist practitioners in implementing her ideas.

1 Why Professional Conversation?

Virtually every educator has experienced the professional rewards that result from rich conversations about practice. Routinely, comments from teachers following a workshop mention that the most positive aspect of the session was the opportunity to engage in dialogue with colleagues. Even when a workshop's nominal purpose is something quite different, for example, observing in classrooms using the framework for teaching, participants report the experience to have been highly rewarding because of the discussions. As they say, "It's all about the conversation." It's through conversation that teachers clarify their beliefs and plans and examine, practice, and consider new possibilities.

Most conversations about teaching are grounded in what has been observed in a classroom, but such conversations can be fruitful even when that is not possible or when the observation is very brief. What is important is that the conversation is enhanced by the skill of those conducting it to dig below the surface, to help teachers examine underlying assumptions and likely consequences of different approaches. With skilled facilitation, conversations can help a teacher reflect deeply on their practice and see patterns of both student behavior and the results of teacher actions.

An essential responsibility of every site administrator is to create a culture of professional inquiry among the faculty. For years, teaching has been characterized by privacy and isolation; it's a reflection of the complexity of teaching and the demands of daily preparation that many teachers don't take the time nor exercise the discipline required to reflect on their own practice and to learn from it. Similarly, they aren't able to either share their expertise with other teachers or learn from that of their colleagues.

> With skilled facilitation, conversations can help a teacher reflect deeply on their practice and see patterns of both student behavior and the results of teacher actions.

Most schools, then, are not learning organizations or professional communities of inquiry. Instead, they are collections of individuals working, under frequently difficult conditions, essentially alone.

And yet the work of teaching is so challenging and so complex that it's essential for teachers to take every opportunity to strengthen their practice. Observations of teaching and professional conversations (among teachers and between teachers and supervisors) are an important vehicle for creating the community of inquiry so essential to ongoing learning.

Many principals report that teachers welcome them in their classrooms, and they report them saying things like "come in any time." Indeed, some teachers express discontent that they see so little of their administrators around the school; these teachers are doing things in their classrooms that they say they would like to show off to their supervisors. But it's unlikely that these sentiments express the full range of emotions experienced by teachers. For many teachers, whenever a supervisor enters a teacher's class, for whatever purpose, the teacher is likely to experience a tightening of the stomach, a visceral fear, that the supervisor will observe something not to his or her liking. They tighten up; the students pick up on the changed chemistry in the room and are likely to shift to good behavior mode. The two—the teacher and the supervisor—do not hold, after all, equal power in the hierarchy of the school; it is a rare teacher who when a principal walks in does not quickly consider what the class looks like through the eyes of a visitor. The result is typically apprehension and anxiety on the part of the teacher.

Even when the teacher has tenure, it is difficult to believe that the observer is not somehow being judgmental; this belief may be even more pronounced when the observer is another teacher. But because of the power differential between teachers and administrators, the anxiety experienced by teachers when an administrator enters the class is likely to be acute. To reduce that anxiety and increase the possibility that professional conversations are productive, it's essential for teachers to know what to expect. This book addresses all these issues, with the aim of helping all educators engage in professional conversations that are as productive as possible.

The Imperative for Improvement in Teaching

It is now accepted wisdom that of all the factors contributing to student learning, schools account for roughly half the differences in student achievement from one student (or groups of students) to another. Other factors include the income and education level of the parents, which exert enormous influence over the stability of a child's upbringing and available opportunities and account for the other half.

But schools themselves are complex systems with many moving parts, such as the richness of the curriculum, the general tone of the school, and the availability of support services and extracurricular activities for students. However, despite these factors, the single most important factor under the control of the school influencing the degree of student learning is the quality of teaching. Thus, a school committed to the improvement of learning must be equally committed to improving the quality of teaching. Such a commitment does not reflect a belief in instructional deficiency. Policymakers and practitioners who advocate professional development for teachers are not arguing that teaching is of poor quality and must be fixed. Not at all; their advocacy for professional development for teachers reflects the recognition that teaching is so *hard* that it is never perfect; no matter how good a lesson is, it could always be improved. As Lee Shulman (2004) has noted, "After 30 years of doing such work, I have concluded that classroom teaching . . . is perhaps the most complex, most challenging, and most demanding, subtle, nuanced, and frightening activity that our species has ever invented" (p. 504).

Furthermore, not only is there an imperative for teaching to improve, this imperative is an ongoing commitment. That is, teachers, like other professionals, must be engaged in a career-long quest to enhance their knowledge and skill; it's not an effort that has been completed by the time teachers have attained a tenured position or have been successful in the profession for a given number of years. That is, professional learning is not an add-on to the daunting responsibilities of teaching; it is *integral to* those responsibilities. The belief that once teachers have completed their preparation programs they are somehow set for their careers is hopelessly outmoded. If it were ever the case, it simply is not today.

The Nature of Teacher Learning

When we understand the importance of ongoing teacher learning for the success of schools, then it's essential to consider how best to promote that learning. This is not a new question; schools have conducted inservice sessions for decades. However, most educators now recognize the ineffectiveness of workshops and presentations in which the teachers' role is a passive one. These are increasingly recognized to be ineffective in improving teacher thinking or changing practice.

When deciding how best to promote teacher learning, it's important to remember that teacher learning is *learning* and that educators can apply what they know about learning to it. Although it's true that adults are different in important respects from children (they have far greater experience, for example) the principles of learning are identical. In a nutshell, what is known

> The single most important factor under the control of the school influencing the degree of student learning is the quality of teaching.

about learning, whether by children or adults, is that learning is done by the *learner* through an active intellectual process. That is, for teachers to learn, it's important for the teacher to be the one doing the intellectual work.

When considered in this light, the limitations of feedback, as typically provided, become evident. From the teacher's standpoint, the experience of listening to suggestions by a supervisor, or even a colleague, is a completely passive one. Indeed, the entire observation/supervision places the teacher in a passive role, and it helps to explain why the typical observation process yields such little value to teachers. In a traditional observation, the supervisor visits the classroom, the supervisor takes notes, the supervisor writes up the observation notes, the supervisor returns, and the supervisor tells the teacher about the lesson. It's important to recognize who is doing the work—the supervisor! Actually, all that's necessary for the teacher is that he or she *endures* the conference; eventually, the supervisor will stop talking and the teacher can leave. Thus, it is scarcely surprising that teachers don't learn much as a consequence of the traditional supervision process; they aren't *doing* anything.

The same may be said of many traditional inservice offerings for teachers, often dismissed as "sit 'n git" sessions. In many of these workshops, which teachers are usually required to attend, an expert, typically from outside the school or district, makes a formal presentation to which teachers listen passively. Even if the workshop is interactive, the activities and the topics addressed are determined by others. Following the session, the teachers return to their classrooms and resume their normal routines—with the workshop materials consigned to the bookshelf. The presenter may indeed be an expert, with important information and insights to share, but teachers are unlikely to learn much from the session if they don't have the opportunity to engage in the difficult work of applying the content to their own situation and context.

Educators have discovered that when they change their approaches to professional learning, they get dramatically different results. In some schools, designated teachers have been trained as instructional coaches and the schedule organized to provide opportunities for them to engage in deep conversations with their colleagues. In other schools, teachers participate in study groups and joint planning. Most of these approaches involve teachers in formal roles, sometimes with a title of department chair or team leader. The role provides them with the mandate to engage their colleagues in conversations about practice, from which important learning can emerge.

Such conversations may also be initiated by administrators and can also yield powerful learning. And because administrators typically have supervisory responsibilities, the conversations carry a subtext of judgment. This unequal distribution of power within a school's organization is one of the realities that must be recognized and is addressed in Chapter 2, "Power and Leadership in Schools." Moreover, an administrator's formal position provides him or her with the natural authority to initiate and sustain discussion on the important concepts that underlie instructional planning and student learning. This issue is addressed in Chapter 3, "The Big Ideas That Shape Professional Conversations." The conversations about teaching are the vehicle through which the school's vision for student learning is both artic- ulated and realized.

Promoting Professional Learning Through Conversation

Of all the approaches available to educators to promote teacher learning, the most powerful (and embedded in virtually all others) is that of professional conversation. Reflective conversations about practice require teachers to understand and analyze events in the classroom. In these conversations, teachers must consider the instructional decisions they have made and examine student learning in light of those decisions.

There can be no doubt that conversation contributes to thinking. Indeed, the English language includes several expressions that attest to the connection: "I'm thinking out loud" (meaning, "I'm saying something, but I'm not exactly sure what it is yet"), or "How do I know what I think until I hear myself say it?" Being challenged to think and express those ideas in words helps people clarify their thoughts.

But the value of professional conversations extends far beyond the particular settings in which they occur; that is, they have value both in the moment and over time. By participat- ing in thoughtful conversations about practice, teachers acquire valuable habits of mind that enable them to pursue such thinking on their own, without the scaffolding provided by the particular conversation. On another occasion, teachers can consider the lessons they have extracted from a given situation and determine their applicability to a new set of circum- stances. It is this transfer of insight that makes professional conversation such a powerful vehicle for learning.

The role of the other (i.e., the colleague, the supervisor, the coach) in the conversation is critical; they supply the mirror, the sounding board, the sympathetic (and indeed some- times challenging) voice. The role of the professional colleague is to engage the teacher in deep conversations about practice. This can only be done if it is informed by an overarching view of learning and teaching and skill in the eliciting teacher thinking. In addition, by inquiring about a teacher's purpose, earlier activities around a topic, and future plans for the class, an observer conveys respect for the teacher's experience and expertise and deep empa- thy for the teacher in the complex decisions that constitute teaching.

But a professional conversation is more than an opportunity to offer support to a teacher engaged in challenging work. It also provides the setting with an agenda and an important opportunity to push at the margins, to promote an examination of underlying principles of learning and teaching. That is, when an observer has spent time, even a short amount of time, in a classroom watching the students' activity and their interactions with one another and with the teacher, the two educators now have something concrete to discuss. They are not talking in theoretical terms only, although their conversation must be grounded in solid theory. The observation enables them to consider whether, for example, a different student grouping, or a slightly modified activity, or a different approach to closure would have yielded greater student engagement or understanding. And when they have actual samples of student work to look at, the richness of these conversations is greatly enhanced.

> This book will assist educators in having powerful conversations about student learning in the context of a shared understanding of the big ideas of learning and motivation that underlie all professional work.

This book, then, is intended to assist educators in having powerful conversations about student learning in the context of a shared understanding of the big ideas of learning and motivation that underlie all professional work.

Assumptions Underlying Professional Conversations

Teaching entails expertise; like other professions, professionalism in teaching requires complex decision making in conditions of uncertainty. Professionalism suggests that there is a body of knowledge about practice, which is embraced by all members of the profession. Therefore, professionals are parts of communities of practice; their teaching is the result of the accumulated wisdom of countless researchers and practitioners whose findings constitute, over time, the accepted theories of action.

To engage in meaningful conversations about practice, educators must establish a common understanding about the nature of the work. Conversations rest on a number of essential assumptions regarding the nature of professionalism in teaching, the importance of ongoing teacher learning, and the mechanisms that promote it.

The Demands of Teaching

As any educator can attest, teaching is enormously complex work involving many dimensions. Particularly for those new to the profession, teaching is daunting in its challenges, and many teachers find themselves ill prepared for their first few years. Compared to other professions, teaching has high rates of attrition; while this is partly explained by modest salaries, it also reflects the demands of the work.

There are several distinct dimensions to the challenges of teaching. First, it's important to recognize that teaching is demanding *physical* work. Teachers are on their feet; they are moving around. Many primary-level teachers are up and down off the floor or at least bending down to be at the same level as their students. Some modern high schools are vast physical structures, and going to one's classroom, then to the lunch room, then to a committee meeting or to the office can involve walking a considerable distance. It's no wonder, then, that most teachers are physically exhausted at the end of a day.

Second, teaching is challenging *emotional* work, and the more caring a teacher is the more demanding his or her work will be. Some students' lives are difficult, and their behavior and performance in school reflect those difficulties. Even when they try to stay removed from students' personal lives, some teachers can't help but be drawn in. Furthermore, teachers have an obligation to step forward if they encounter evidence of serious deprivation or actual abuse. All this takes a toll on teachers as well; they can find themselves quite exhausted from the emotional demands of their work.

But most important, teaching is demanding *cognitive* work; teachers make hundreds of nonroutine decisions each day. Shulman (2004) has described the intellectual demands of teaching brilliantly:

> The practice of teaching involves a far more complex task environment than does that of medicine. The teacher is confronted not with a single patient but with a classroom filled with 25–35 youngsters. The teacher's goals are multiple; the school's obligations far from unitary. Even in the ubiquitous primary reading group, the teacher must simultaneously be concerned with the learning of decoding skills as well as comprehension, with motivation and love of reading as well as word attack, and must both monitor the performance of the six or eight students in front of her while not losing touch with the other two dozen in the room. Moreover, individual differences among pupils are a fact of life, exacerbated even further by the worthwhile policies of mainstreaming and school integration. The only time a physician could possibly encounter a situation of comparable complexity would be in the emergency room of a hospital during or after a natural disaster. (p. 258)

This cognitive characteristic of teaching has enormous implications, of course, in how teachers engage in conversations about practice. If one acknowledges, as one must, the cognitive nature of teaching, then conversations about teaching must be about *the cognition*. It's not sufficient to describe, or discuss, or even critique what a teacher has done; it's essential also to explore the reasoning that underlie those actions. And as part of exploring the thinking, educators will also be involved, inevitably, in considerations about alternative courses of actions and the likely consequences of each.

Of course, recognizing the cognitive nature of teaching implies supporting the ongoing development of such thinking.

> Conversations about teaching must be about *the cognition*. It's not sufficient to describe, or discuss, or even critique what a teacher has done; it's essential also to explore the reasoning that underlie those actions.

This is explained powerfully by Carl D. Glickman, Stephen P. Gordan, and Jovita M. Ross-Gordan (2003).

> The problem with the need for high-stage teachers is that, although the work by its nature demands autonomous and flexible thinking, teachers in most schools are not supported in ways to improve their thinking. The only alternative for a teacher in a complex environment who cannot adjust to multiple demands and is not being helped to acquire the abilities to think abstractly and autonomously is to *simplify and deaden the instructional environment.* Teachers make the environment less complex by disregarding differences among students and by establishing routines and instructional practices that remain the same day after day and year after year. . . . Effective teaching has been misunderstood and misapplied as a set and sequence of certain teaching behaviors (review previous day's objectives, present objectives, explain, demonstrate, guided practice, check for understanding, etc.) This explanation of effectiveness is simply untrue. (p. 72)

The Contextual Nature of Teaching

Teachers don't exercise their professional expertise in isolation, either from their colleagues or their setting. All teaching, in other words, occurs within a context, even if one is referring to the same discipline at the same level, for example, third-grade mathematics. The essential mathematics concepts to be learned may be essentially the same in all third-grade classes, but students from a rural environment will be able to understand those concepts in light of fencing on a farm, for example, or the need to mix animal feed in certain proportions. Students who live in a city would find other references more meaningful, such as the distance traveled on a city bus or the dimensions of a local playground. Thus, the techniques teachers use and the examples they employ are adapted to the context in which they are working.

The Danielson framework for teaching describes the essential work of teaching, dividing that work into twenty-two components grouped into four broad domains (planning and preparation, the classroom environment, instruction, and professional responsibilities). Each component (such as establishing an environment of respect and rapport) is described with the description followed by a chart or a rubric, which identifies the critical elements of that component and then provides brief descriptions of a teacher's performance at each of four levels of performance (unsatisfactory, basic, proficient, and distinguished).

The framework for teaching is itself generic; that is, there is one framework that encompasses all teaching situations, from first-grade literacy to high school physics. This is not to dismiss the range of factors (the age and culture of the students, the subject being addressed, the setting—whether urban, suburban, or rural) that make each educational encounter unique. But beneath the unique character of each situation are fundamental constructs; in every successful classroom, students feel respected, for example, by both the teacher and other students. The specific actions taken by a high school teacher to create such a culture may be profoundly different from those taken by a first-grade teacher. And yet the result is the same: every student honored, respected, and valued.

However, the fact remains that teaching is highly contextualized; conversations about practice concern the events of a single teaching episode with a specific group of students learning some specific content. How an individual addresses those particularities is part of the skill of teaching and may be explored through conversation. A teacher will use slightly different approaches with one group of students than another, even when teaching similar content. In deciding which approach to take, a teacher demonstrates both expertise and sensitivity to each situation. And exploring the teacher's thinking in deciding on each approach is one of the factors that makes such conversations rich and productive.

The Role of Feedback

The place of feedback in learning has been well established, particularly for students. It is pointed out that when students receive feedback that is timely and specific, against clear standards, they are able to bridge the gap between current performance and desired goals more quickly than when the feedback is general or delayed in time from their work. That is, feedback in the form of "Great effort!" or "You can do better!" does little to guide students in how their work could be improved. To stimulate additional effort and successful performance by students, teachers must be able to show students, specifically, how their efforts fall short and what they must do to bring their work up to meet the standard.

Similarly, feedback must be given in a timely fashion. When a test is returned to students several weeks after the event, many of them will have forgotten the details of what they were learning and will find it difficult to make the necessary effort to correct their errors in understanding or procedures. By then the content is cold, and it's much more difficult to make use of even thoughtful teacher comments than it would have been closer to the event.

The biggest gains in student learning occur when students assess and monitor their own performance against clear performance standards. When they examine, for example, a sample of their—or a peer's—writing against a rubric and determine that it falls short in some aspect (such as clarity of language), the author is better able to address the difficulty and strengthen the effort.

Much of the same reasoning applies to teachers. When there are clear standards of practice, feedback against those standards enables teachers to improve their performance. It is this phenomenon that has made the framework for teaching so widely used among educators around the world; teachers are able to receive specific information about their practice and to see what they must do to improve. New teachers, in particular, appreciate hearing from an administrator that their performance is on the right track, and they value a supervisor's praise for using some excellent practices. Such feedback is validating and goes a long way toward motivating educators in their first years of teaching, when many become discouraged by the complexity of the work.

But as teachers gain experience and become more mature in their practice, they become less reliant on pats on the back from administrators. Especially when teachers have attained the security of a continuing contract position, they are able to become more self-reliant in assessing their own practice and in charting a course toward improvement. They are aware of where their teaching needs to be strengthened, and they are able to pursue a course of action toward it. Furthermore, when teachers participate in professional learning communities, they work together to solve challenging educational challenges. Thus, experienced teachers don't rely nearly as much as do novices on the positive strokes they receive from administrators; instead, they work as colleagues to devise better instructional approaches for their students. The administrator's role, then, particularly with experienced teachers, in conducting professional conversations is more that of colleague than that of external judge.

This way of looking at professional conversations has implications for the way administrators offer feedback to teachers. Supervisors have learned, in their preparation programs, that a critical function of supervision is the observation of teaching and the providing of feedback. And as already noted, teachers early in their career appreciate such feedback from administrators because it affirms their efforts. But for more experienced teachers, feedback can actually seem patronizing and condescending; they are experienced professionals; what they seek from their administrators is the counsel of an even more experienced colleague, not a pat on the back from an individual who may not be as familiar with the details of the teacher's instructional situation as is the teacher.

Thus, feedback plays a smaller role in professional conversations than it does in more traditional forms of supervision and professional development. When educators recognize that for teachers to advance in their understanding, they must be the ones to engage in the work of self-assessment and reflection on practice, then external feedback is even seen as a possible hindrance to that process.

Summary

Professional conversation is an essential technique to promote professional learning among teachers. These conversations may be undertaken by teachers and administrators, teachers and formal teacher leaders (such as instructional coaches), or among teachers as colleagues. In all cases, they are conducted in such a way to respect the professional judgment of teachers and as a vehicle to explore ways to enhance student learning.

Professional conversations about teaching are embedded in the complex nature of teaching and reflect important assumptions about teaching: the nature of professionalism, the demands of professional learning, and the appropriate role of feedback. In addition, such conversations provide an opportunity to explore the nature of student learning in specific situations.

> When educators recognize that for teachers to advance in their understanding, they must be the ones to engage in the work of self-assessment and reflection on practice, then external feedback is even seen as a possible hindrance to that process.

Furthermore, conversations about practice are grounded in important big ideas about student learning and take place within the organizational context of schools. In particular, administrators hold greater raw power than do teachers, and this fact colors all professional conversations. These issues are explored in the chapters that follow.

2   Power and Leadership in Schools

Professional conversations in schools—between teachers and administrators and among teaching colleagues—occur within the context of the school's organizational structure. In that structure, the principal is the designated leader of the school; teachers work, to at least some extent, under the direction of the principal. And yet, teachers, no less than administrators, are professionals. They have engaged in professional training and preparation. They have acquired considerable expertise, both about the subjects they teach and how best to teach those subjects to students. There is, then, an inevitable tension between the professionalism of teachers and the authority of administrators; resolving that tension is the task of this chapter. That is, just because some individuals, notably principals, hold greater power in the school's structure than do teachers, it is not the case that professional conversations among teachers and administrators cannot be collegial. They can and must be both collegial and professionally rewarding.

Overview

In schools, as in other professional organizations, conflicting ideas with respect to power and leadership are forced to coexist. In the private sector, no such ambiguity is necessary; the CEO is the boss at the top of a well-defined organizational chart with reporting lines clearly specified. There is no uncertainty as to who is in charge; decisions are made at the apex and are communicated downward. If a subordinate wants to take initiative about, for example, a new procedure, it is clear to whom a presentation must be made and who will approve the plan. Modern writers in business leadership argue, to be sure, that power tempered by a concern for the dynamics of collaborative work can yield better relationships and better results than a hard-nosed approach. But, for all that, there is no ambiguity as to where the power resides.

In fact, CEOs of business organizations report a considerable culture shock when they enter the world of nonprofit organizations. They find that, whereas in the business world they were able to implement policy simply by announcing it, it is no longer possible. In fact, an interesting perspective is offered by Philip Lader, whose career has spanned both the private sector (most recently the chairman of WPP group) as well as positions in government and the nonprofit sector (president of universities in the United States and Australia). The following is how he described his experience as ambassador to the Court of St. James (in London) from 1997 to 2001:

> There you are at the helm of the great ship, with everyone scurrying about. Only after about four months of steering the wheel do you realize that it is not connected to the rudder. Everyone is saluting you and saying 'aye-aye,' as they then go below and steer the ship themselves. (Lader quoted in Silverman & Taliento, 2005, p. 4)

But even in the business community, as Warren Bennis (2003) has pointed out,

> The "Lone Ranger" is dead. To lead a great group, a leader need not possess all the individual skills of the group members. What he or she must have is vision, the ability to rally the others, and integrity. . . . Such leaders also need superb curatorial and coaching skills—an eye for talent, the ability to recognize correct choices, contagious optimism, a gift for bringing out the best in others, the ability to facilitate communication and mediate conflict, a sense of fairness, and, as always, the authenticity and integrity that creates trust. (p. xix)

In schools, as in many other organizations, power and leadership are intertwined, and, to some extent, at odds with one another. In fact, occasionally they collide. Therefore, for administrators and supervisors to exercise leadership, they must appreciate the interlocking demands of their roles as the individual in whom the authority of the organization resides and the complex matter of exercising leadership in a professional organization.

Leadership in schools, as in other nonprofit organizations, depends not on fiat but on consensus. Reynold Levy (a senior officer of AT&T, as well as president of the Lincoln Center for the Performing Arts and former president of the International Rescue Committee) described the experience of Steve Trachtenberg, the president of George Washington University. According to Levy,

> To get any major decision of consequence made at GWU he needs seven green lights. And every time he gets six and turns to the left he finds that number two is now

blinking yellow. He's got to go back over to that and switch it on to make it green. And so he needs to get those green lights fixed long enough so that his board can look at them and be assured that he can then move forward. (quoted in Silverman & Taliento, 2005, p. 5)

This need for consensus building is a hallmark of professional organizations, which sets them apart from the corporate world. As one who made the shift from the for-profit to the nonprofit sector put it, reflecting some frustration, "It's not like the mail room guy has to weigh in . . . there has to be an end to it" (Levy quoted in Silverman & Taliento, 2005, pp. 5–6).

Schools are more like nonprofit organizations than they are like corporate entities. Teachers are skilled with professional training and experience, in some cases extensive. Furthermore, because most teachers remain in their schools longer than do principals, teachers tend to be the custodians of the institution's memory and culture. They maintain the rituals; they know how things are done. Although practices may be changed, it is typically a slow process and one not always directed by principals. That is, educational rhetoric notwithstanding principals are not always able to perform the function of educational leader envisioned by management theory; their jobs entail enormous responsibility— ensuring, among other things, that the building runs smoothly, that students are safe and supervised, that budgets and reports are submitted accurately and on time, and that parents are heard. However, as will be discussed below, although principals are nominally the leader of the building, including in instructional matters, they are not necessarily the most expert, and this reality influences how power is exercised.

The Reality of Power

As noted above, professional conversations occur within the context of the school's hierarchical structure, which reflects differential amounts of power held by different individuals; educators must recognize this reality as they strive to create and maintain a culture of professional inquiry. Principals and supervisors have the formal power in schools; the principal's office is where the buck stops. When a member of the public or an official from the central office needs to communicate with the school, it is to the principal that the request is made. There are other power centers in the school, for example, teachers to whom their colleagues look for direction and expertise, secretaries whose opinion carries weight in matters of school operations, or leaders of the parent organization who expect to vet many decisions. But pure, raw power, resides with principals and their designees.

> Although principals are nominally the leader of the building, including in instructional matters, they are not necessarily the most expert, and this reality influences how power is exercised.

The reality of power has enormous implications in all aspects of the school and how it operates. In the matter of personnel evaluation and particularly with respect to probationary teachers, the principal's (or designee's) power is essentially unlimited. A probationary teacher's contract (in virtually all jurisdictions) is renewed or not renewed solely on the recommendation of the administrator, frequently with no cause needing to be cited. It is sufficient for a principal to decide to not renew a contract.

With tenured teachers, on the other hand, most contracts impose significant restrictions on an administrator's exercise of raw (some would say arbitrary) power. Although teachers may be dismissed for incompetence, the procedures that must be followed are detailed and are designed to protect teachers from being punished for such things as their political activities, for example. However, even with the protections afforded them, tenured teachers may feel insecure when an administrator enters their rooms. The very presence of an administrator makes many teachers nervous, and their behavior changes. Similarly, even motorists driving within a speed limit may remove their foot from the pedal when they spot a police car lurking on the shoulder. This is the reality of power, and it is, to some extent, incompatible with the characteristics of a culture of professional inquiry so essential for professional leadership and ongoing learning by teachers.

The challenge, then, for an entire staff and, in particular, administrators, is to understand the nature of true leadership and its relationship with power. The situation in schools, like other professional organizations, presents a particular paradox; of course, teachers may possess greater expertise about the subjects they teach or the developmental nature of their students than do the administrators by whom they are nominally supervised. It's not hard to describe the type of administrator who exercises power in an irresponsible manner, a manner that undercuts the expertise of teachers and undermines staff morale. Such administrators appear to relish power for its own sake: "Because I said so" is a sufficient explanation for a decision. Such exercise of power does not constitute leadership; teachers feel they are working in a dictatorship and take their first opportunity to transfer to another school.

Leadership in a Professional Organization

To serve as a successful school leader, it is essential to understand the dual nature of leadership in professional organizations. On the one hand, schools possess many of the hierarchical characteristics of a bureaucracy; one of those characteristics is that there is a final resting place for the proverbial buck. Someone must be in charge and see to it that operational procedures are in place and decisions are taken in a timely fashion. At the very least, a school must be well run.

On the other hand, as noted above, teachers are professionals in their own right; they may possess considerable expertise and enjoy deep respect among their colleagues for their skill. Naturally, not all teachers are so endowed, presenting school leaders with the challenge of supplying guidance to those teachers who need it, while, assuming more of a support role for those who don't. And perhaps, most challenging of all, they need to determine which teachers are which—that is, which teachers will benefit from ongoing guidance and direction and which merely need support.

There is another issue as well. Even a school populated exclusively by star teachers—that is, those who are expert in the subjects they teach and the related pedagogy and in the nature of the students they teach—will not be a great organization without consensus on the broad principles of learning and a vision for structuring professional decisions. It's not sufficient for a school to be comprised of individual expertise; that expertise must be mobilized in the service of a common vision. This, then, is the challenge of educational leadership. How do the formal leaders of schools (principally administrators) exercise their leadership in such a way that they respect the complexity of teaching and the expertise of teachers while simultaneously increasing awareness and skill on the part of an entire staff regarding the nature of student learning and how to promote it?

A powerful analogy may be found among professional musicians. A musician must be highly skilled to secure a position with, for example, the Cleveland Orchestra; the violinist, oboist, or percussionist must demonstrate both technical fluency with his or her instrument and familiarity with the symphonic repertoire. However, once a member of the orchestra, that same clarinetist does not decide which pieces to play; the musical director determines, for example, that the program will include Beethoven and Prokofiev. Nor is the expert clarinetist free to play a Beethoven symphony in, for instance, the style of Gershwin. All members of the orchestra (although experts in playing their own instruments) must adhere to the purposes of the conductor and use their skill to execute certain pieces of music according to the conductor's vision of those masterworks. The conductor does far more than keep the beat; during rehearsals, the orchestra learns to play the different selections providing the sound that reflects the conductor's vision.

However, that same clarinetist might also be a member of a jazz ensemble. And although the fundamentals of playing the clarinet are the same as in a symphony orchestra, many specific techniques used are different. Furthermore, in a jazz ensemble, not only are musicians free to improvise, they are expected to do so; those improvisations, at specified times, are at the heart of jazz. There is, in both music and teaching, an inevitable tension between individual expertise and collective purpose. So although all members of the orchestra are truly masters of their instruments, they use their skills in the service of the collective

> Even a school populated exclusively by star teachers—that is, those who are expert in the subjects they teach and the related pedagogy and in the nature of the students they teach—will not be a great organization without consensus on the broad principles of learning and a vision for structuring professional decisions.

effort of the orchestra as a whole. Similarly, when teachers work together in a school, they use their expertise in the service of the school's mission and vision, usually as articulated by the principal.

But a site administrator, for all the authority vested in the position, does not exercise complete discretion. A principal does not exercise power by fiat; he or she cannot simply declare that a certain practice will be implemented. (Actually, a principal *could* make such a declaration, thereby guaranteeing that either the effort would be sabotaged or it would result in the undermining of morale among the faculty, whose members would feel that their professional expertise was not being respected.)

Rather, a school leader must exercise softer leadership skills, a focus on vision and purpose, persuasion, appeals to professional ethics, and dialogue that engages teachers in a problem-solving approach to the multiple challenges facing their schools. When necessary, for example, when faced with a threat, a school administrator may revert to an authoritarian style, but for maximum benefit, the administrator is both an inspirational and a capable leader, one respected by members of the faculty and larger community as both professional and caring.

What are the components of a school leader's repertoire? How does a site administrator help a school become more effective in engaging all students in learning important content? How does a school leader mobilize the entire faculty of a school around the most recent research on human learning and motivation to yield maximum results?

Exhibiting Professional Competence

School leaders must be respected for their professional knowledge and skill; they must stay abreast of developments in the research into teaching and learning and be able to engage with members of their faculties about the implications of such new understandings. Of course, teachers are the closest to the ground in the specific details of the subjects they teach, and it is their responsibility to keep their knowledge current. But they must also have confidence that the instructional leaders in their school are sufficiently knowledgeable that they can guide the conversation and that they are able to help teachers translate new findings into concrete practices.

> School leaders must be respected for their professional knowledge and skill; they must stay abreast of developments in the research into teaching and learning and be able to engage with members of their faculties about the implications of such new understandings.

School administrators must, of course, be capable managers; it's essential that a school function smoothly and that the school's infrastructure be well established and maintained, with clear procedures for decision making, rotations of responsibilities, engagement of parent councils, and the like. Indeed, the principal's job has become ever larger and the centerpiece of most school improvement efforts. As such, it's impossible for them to stay on top of every detail of the curriculum and how teachers engage students with it. But they must have command of the big ideas, the overarching principles that define teaching and learning in the school, and they must retain their focus uncompromisingly on issues to do with student learning. Teachers must have confidence that site administrators are sufficiently well informed and can exercise good judgment in sufficient measure to steer the ship, sometimes even in choppy waters. In contrast, teachers can't be expected to put their trust in an individual whom they consider ignorant, or self-serving, or simply trying to look good in others' eyes.

Somewhat paradoxically, an aspect of professional competence is humility. Respected leaders are not afraid to admit that they were wrong about something; such honesty conveys a basic humanity, an awareness of one's own fallibility. Consistency in the face of resistance may reflect strength, but persistence when confronted with negative evidence is more likely to be simple stubbornness. Thus, flexibility and the willingness to learn from others are both traits that signal instructional leadership. But professional competence also, at times, requires maintaining the focus of all educators on the important principles of teaching and learning and not permitting them to be distracted by the shifting winds of fashion.

Establishing Trust

The first, and some would argue the most important, characteristic of a school making progress toward improved student learning is that the leader has established an atmosphere of trust: trust among teachers and between teachers and administrators. Many researchers (Arneson, 2014; Bennis, 2003; Costa & Garmston, 2002; Tschannen-Moran, 2004; Whitaker, Whitaker, & Lumpa, 2000) have analyzed the nature of trust, and although the different descriptions vary to some extent, there is general consensus as to its elements.

For starters, trusted leaders act with consistency. Leaders don't act arbitrarily; they don't change their minds based on the latest fad. Teachers, in other words, can count on them. This does not mean that they are not open-minded when faced with new evidence or recent research findings. But they do not behave capriciously; teachers can rely on them to act consistently in pursuing the school's mission. Good leaders don't blow hot and cold; they are steady and reliable.

In addition, respected administrators maintain confidentiality. Teachers can count on their leaders to not betray information about their concerns with respect to students, colleagues, or their personal lives. Trust in a leader includes confidence that

> The first, and some would argue the most important, characteristic of a school making progress toward improved student learning is that the leader has established an atmosphere of trust: trust among teachers and between teachers and administrators.

information discussed in confidence will remain safe unless explicit permission has been granted to share it with others.

Last and probably most important, trusted leaders protect others' vulnerability. At its most basic level, trust involves exposing oneself to possible harm. In the hierarchical organization of schools, teachers cannot entirely trust an administrator when they fear that something told in confidence may be held against them. For example, a teacher will be less inclined to ask for assistance with a student if she fears that the episode will resurface in an evaluation report that the teacher cannot control her class. In other words, trusting another person requires taking a risk, in which the possibility of betrayal always lurks.

In hierarchical organizations such as schools, it is the obligation of the individual with the greater power to assume the responsibility of building and sustaining trusting relationships. The leader must earn the trust of teachers by behaving in ways that convey a safe environment for risk taking. Just as teachers in their classrooms must build an environment within which students are held to high standards but can experiment with thoughts and ideas, principals must create a school culture of both high professional expectations and respect for the views of all. This is done through a slow process of engaging in meaningful dialogue with teachers, being reliable and consistent, and never betraying confidences. Each instance of trustworthy behavior on the part of the leader contributes to the development of trust between teachers and the principal.

However, there is an asymmetry with respect to trust; although trust develops slowly, it can be destroyed (or at least seriously undermined) very quickly. Many people have experienced the troubling phenomenon of discovering that an individual one thought could be trusted cannot. When this happens, it may be a long time before one is prepared to take a risk again.

Of course, building trust is not a one-way process; teachers must also earn the trust of their administrators. They also must act consistently and hold confidences secure. But it is the nature of unequal power that the consequences of a betrayal of trust are more severe for the individual with less power. This is yet one more reason why informal conversations are critical to the culture in a school; they help convey respect and build trust across the hierarchy.

Reconciling Power and Leadership

It's essential for educational leaders who intend to influence their schools to thread their way through the sometimes conflicting impulses of power and collegial leadership. What is the role, in other words, of the leader in a professional organization such as a school? What should the leader actually *do* to exercise power in a responsible and professional manner? How are these actions enhanced and reflected in professional conversations? There are several essential answers to this question, which are outlined below.

Creating the Vision: Establishing the Big Ideas

All organizations, whether they acknowledge it or not, are influenced by a governing vision, an ideology, a sense of what is possible. Throughout the 20th century, the assembly line model held sway, in which it was assumed that knowledge was poured into passive students as they progressed through the days and years. And furthermore, some students were believed to be capable of holding a great deal of knowledge, others capable of holding very little. Such concepts die hard; for educational leaders to convince professional colleagues of a new approach to the biggest questions affecting the school—the matter of the governing vision—they must be armed with compelling research evidence and powers of persuasion.

School leaders understand very well that schools undertake an essential societal function, namely to prepare an educated citizenry for the demands of both employment and citizenship. These demands are more fully explored in Chapter 3, "The Big Ideas That Shape Professional Conversations." The vision for a school consists of more than the high-level demands of contemporary society; it includes the notion that achieving such high levels of performance is within the grasp of virtually every child in the school. A visionary leader reminds teachers that children are born naturally curious, and motivated by the drive for competence and independence. It is one of the paradoxes of an educational system that although there are no intellectually lazy four-year-olds, there are many intellectually lazy fourteen-year-olds. Granted, much happens in children's lives between the ages of four and fourteen, but one of the principal things that happens is that they go to school. Educators must examine this phenomenon carefully and be prepared to face the brutal possibility that schools themselves may be contributing to many children's decrease in intellectual curiosity. The issue of learning, and recent research findings concerning it, is addressed in Chapter 3; it is sufficient for the examination of the school's vision to point out that an essential characteristic of leadership is to paint a compelling picture of what schools can accomplish and why it is important to do so. This is not a new idea. One of the pioneers of organizational development, Chester Barnard (1958), pointed out that "the inculcation of belief in the real existence of a common purpose is an essential executive function" (quoted in Sergiovanni, 1992, p. 72).

Purposing

Related to creating a vision, educational leaders are also able to help teachers recognize their place in that vision. One of the powerful skills of visionary leaders, one that motivates ordinary people to extraordinary accomplishments, is the ability to convey a sense of larger purpose, the ability to help people see the

> The vision for a school consists of more than the high-level demands of contemporary society; it includes the notion that achieving such high levels of performance is within the grasp of virtually every child in the school.

(sometimes rather mundane) aspects of their work in light of a compelling purpose, a higher calling. As Michael Feiner (2004) has written,

> High-performance leaders believe that they will change the world, and they infuse their subordinates with this belief. When a leader provides meaning and purpose with this degree of fervor, with this sense of passion and significance to the future of the human race, he or she convinces people that they are *building a cathedral, not cutting stone.* (p. 43; italics in original)

Similarly, leaders at FedEx constantly remind people that they're delivering the most important commerce in the history of the world: "You're not delivering sand and gravel. You're delivering someone's pacemaker, chemotherapy treatment for cancer drugs, the part that keeps the F-18's flying, or the legal brief that decides the case" (Fred Smith quoted in Feiner, 2004, p. 107).

Of course, it is the vision and purpose of schools that attracts many into the teaching profession; they are making an important contribution to the lives of children and to the future of society. It is this sense of larger purpose that pulls many from the private sector into teaching following a successful career. "People would rather be here than working for some snow tire company," writes Bill Novelli, currently the CEO of AARP. And quoting an employee at Levi Strauss, he added, "I don't want it to say on my tombstone that I shipped a million pairs of jeans" (quoted in Silverman & Taliento, 2005, p. 13).

The role of the leader, then, is not only to articulate the idea system that governs actions in a school, but to inspire others to see their role in carrying out and being connected to these ideas. The idea system, the big ideas of Chapter 3, constitute the architecture underlying specific actions in the school, the "values and structures to which individuals can adhere . . . once in place, an idea structure constitutes the basis of a leadership practice based on professional and moral authority" (Sergiovanni, 1992, p. 71).

Sergiovanni (1992) further points out that in a professional organization the traditional hierarchy of the school is upended; it is not the principal who is at the apex, nor the students and teachers. Rather, that position is reserved for the ideas, values, and commitments that are the basis for professional relationships. When viewed in this manner, with the ideas and commitments as the organizing principle, then the leader's role is transformed into that of articulating those ideas and commitments and in facilitating the work of problem solving as to the best way to make them a reality. When the big ideas are the highest authority, then the principals and supervisors can be problem solvers. Teachers don't

> The role of the leader, then, is not only to articulate the idea system that governs actions in a school, but to inspire others to see their role in carrying out and being connected to these ideas.

do something because they are directed to do so by their superior but because it is more likely to fulfill the school's vision, and will result in important student learning.

Creating and Sustaining a Learning Organization

Just as teachers have the responsibility to create a culture for learning in their classrooms, school leaders must establish a culture of professional inquiry among the faculty. That is, it's not sufficient that teachers be expert in their work; they must, as members of a profession, constantly seek to improve their skills. Teacher preparation and training, as in other fields, is merely the beginning of professional learning, which can be expected to continue throughout one's career. The imperative for continuing learning by teachers is not because teaching is deficient; rather, it is that teaching is so *hard* that it is never perfect and can always be improved.

It should be noted that many schools are the antithesis of a learning organization. Teachers are physically isolated from one another, and the schedules of most schools don't permit time for teachers to engage in ongoing professional collaboration. Nor is such joint planning and mutual learning part of the professional culture in many schools. Rather, teachers believe themselves to be, and are treated as, independent contractors; although some of them are highly skilled at their craft, they work essentially in isolation. Furthermore, any request to visit a class, whether by a supervisor or fellow teacher, is regarded as a thinly veiled indication of inadequacy.

A component of a culture of professional inquiry is openness to change. Successful schools do not become frozen in old practices; the educators in them recognize the need for flexibility in achieving their goals. The new approaches to be used, or tried, are naturally informed by the results of professional inquiry—that is, they are grounded in the examination of evidence. But in addition, there is a cultural openness to the quest for better ways of doing things, ways that might represent a significant departure from past practice.

For teachers to engage in significant professional inquiry, structures must be established to make collaboration possible. But it is more than a matter of scheduling: It is a matter of values. Teachers and administrators must all accept that ongoing learning is not an add-on to the work of teaching. Rather, it is *integral* to that work. Teaching is highly complex work, with much yet to be learned. A commitment to ongoing professional learning, within a culture of inquiry, is critical to high levels of student performance. Establishing and maintaining such a culture is central to the work of both administrative and teacher leadership.

In a learning organization, every member of the organization is engaged in learning; in schools, this suggests that although teacher learning is at the heart of it, administrators,

A commitment to ongoing professional learning, within a culture of inquiry, is critical to high levels of student performance. Establishing and maintaining such a culture is central to the work of both administrative and teacher leadership.

the office staff, and teaching assistants must also be engaged in efforts to improve their knowledge and skill. Although this is an obvious statement, it is frequently overlooked. Furthermore, when promoting a learning organization, it is essential to apply what is known about all learning, namely that it occurs through the active participation of the learner. Hence, if a school leader intends to establish a learning organization and promote the learning of teachers, teachers must be active agents in that process. A learning organization is not something imposed by fiat or by administrative authority; instead, it is cultivated through an unwavering focus on the school's vision, using insights from the big ideas described in Chapter 3.

Using Positional Authority to Promote Good Teaching

Principals are required by law to ensure good teaching, and to that end, they observe teachers' classroom practice, examine artifacts (such as parent newsletters and planning documents), and conduct conferences with teachers. These activities are sometimes conducted in a top-down, punitive manner that shuts down teacher learning. Alternatively, they may be conducted in such a manner as to maximize thoughtfulness on the part of teachers. Procedures that enhance teacher learning, in other words, may be incorporated into even an otherwise traditional system of teacher evaluation.

It is a reality that when an administrator enters a teacher's room, the atmosphere changes; both the teacher and the administrator know that the principal holds authority in the evaluation of teachers. Such evaluations must be conducted in the context of a shared understanding of practice and purpose. Furthermore, if teachers have ample and genuine opportunities for self-assessment, reflection on practice, and professional conversation, these evaluations will enable teachers to engage in deep professional learning.

Most evaluations of teaching occur in somewhat formal ways: Classroom observations are scheduled, teachers prepare for them, and students may be instructed to be on their best behavior. Even in this formal setting, however, the conferences that follow a scheduled observation may be conducted in such a manner to elicit the teacher's thinking about the lesson, the success of different portions of it, and what might have been done differently to make it even more effective.

But it is the conversations following brief, unscheduled classroom visits that have the potential to spark valuable professional conversations. Tom Peters and Nancy Austin (1985) in *A Passion for Excellence: The Leadership Difference* coined the phrase "management by wandering around." In the business literature, this term refers to the leader's practice of being out and about, being visible in the cubicles and on the shop floor. By being around, by inquiring of subordinates how things are going, by soliciting ideas, the manager has his or her finger on the pulse of the organization and can make small adjustments in a timely manner.

In a school setting, management by wandering around implies dropping in on classrooms, talking frequently with students and teachers, and discussing issues in the faculty room. These informal conversations lend themselves to exploring the implications of the big ideas for practice in engaging in joint problem solving. Such brief visits may well constitute part of a school's evaluation process, but because they are unscheduled, the lessons themselves are likely to be more representative of a teacher's practice than are the scheduled ones. Therefore, both teacher and administrator know that the teaching episode observed reflects the teacher's authentic practice; when these are conducted in an environment of trust and respect, they offer important opportunities for professional learning.

Serving as Coach

When a culture of professional inquiry has been established, teachers will naturally regard their principal as a resource to assist in strengthening practice. This coaching is most likely to exist between administrators and experienced teachers, who are secure in their position. Teachers have access to others as coaches, including other teachers, instructional coaches, and department chairs. But coaching, conducted by teachers or administrators, is an important opportunity to improve teaching.

In a coaching relationship between a teacher and administrator, the teacher initiates contact with the administrator around a specific aspect of practice. The administrator then visits the teacher's classroom to provide another set of eyes, perhaps to collect data on, for example, whether the teacher is inadvertently excluding a group of students from a class discussion.

Coaching conversations between teachers and administrators are nonevaluative, and because they are initiated by the teacher, the administrator's role is purely one of support. But of course, because of a principal's positional authority, teachers must feel secure in their positions before they will take such initiative. They must also believe that they are working in a truly professional environment, one in which the environment is safe for risk taking. When those conditions are met, when the principal has established a culture of professional inquiry, then the door is open for productive coaching conversations even across lines of power and authority.

Summary

As in other professional organizations, the exercise of positional authority in schools must be reconciled with the demands of leadership. Teachers are, after all, professionals; they possess considerable professional expertise. On the other hand, the organization of schools requires that someone be in charge, that the buck stop somewhere. Leadership in schools, therefore, is a complex matter and does not rest simply on the authority vested in the principal. It also requires, on the part of principals, expertise and vision and the more subtle skills of collaboration, facilitation, and professional conversation.

A school is more than a collection of its teachers, regardless of how capable they are. In seeking to elevate a school's offerings for its students, in enhancing the learning experiences available on a daily basis, school leaders must use their positional authority to set the tone and vision and to assist teachers in examining their practice against that vision. The content of that tone and vision, together with the skills of professional conversation, are the subjects of subsequent chapters of this book.

3 The Big Ideas That Shape Professional Conversations

It was noted in Chapter 2, "Power and Leadership in Schools," that one of the most important uses of positional authority is to forge consensus among a professional staff regarding the big ideas that shape everyday practice. As you will see here as well as in the chapters that follow, commitment for a consensus on these big ideas can serve as the underpinnings for professional conversation. But what are those big ideas, what is the research on which they are based, and why are they important?

Ideas are powerful. They help us make sense of the world, and they enable us to determine the best approach in a given situation. Furthermore, ideas shape our notions of what is *right* and whether or not a situation is acceptable. When students from different ethnic backgrounds enroll at very different rates, for example, in advanced courses, educators' acceptance reflects a host of other beliefs about intelligence, student preparation, and the capability of different students for challenging work. When students of all levels are subjected to day after day of memorization of facts and practice of procedures, those instructional approaches reflect numerous beliefs about the nature of what is to be learned and the optimal strategies to produce that learning. The big ideas described in this chapter include the following:

- What constitutes important learning?
- What causes learning?
- How are students motivated?
- What is intelligence, and how do students' views influence their actions?

Every educator goes about his or her daily work with a complex set of beliefs, assumptions, and values, many of which are only partially acknowledged. These mental models inform everyday practice and govern, to a large extent, the multiple decisions that result in practice. These mental models are grounded in the experiences of individuals from earliest childhood through their entire schooling, their professional preparation, their experiences in teaching, and their interactions with colleagues. Thus, the complex set of beliefs that underlie decisions about practice result in an elaborate web of norms and expectations, which are, in most cases, unexamined.

Teaching, as James Stigler and James Hiebert (1999) have pointed out, is, among other things, a cultural activity. That is, "doing school" is surrounded by norms and expectations regarding what happens there and how the interactions between teacher and students are structured. By virtue of having gone to school, teachers absorb these cultural norms; changing them can constitute a significant challenge for a school's professional community. And yet prevailing views are increasingly recognized to be counterproductive in enabling schools to achieve the results for which they aim.

Leaders, therefore, whether administrators or teachers, have a deep responsibility to ensure that the big ideas at work in their schools are those that are supported by research and that will yield the most positive outcomes for students. The challenge is to promote these ideas even when they digress from so-called accepted wisdom of both the educational establishment and the community at large. It is always important to articulate such ideas explicitly, but particularly so when they are not widely understood. Furthermore, it would be astonishing if an entire faculty was comprised of individuals who held identical views regarding these important issues. So the leadership challenge involves not only seeking the best information and theories about learning but forging consensus among members of a school's professional staff.

For schools to be truly research based and grounded in best practices, a thorough understanding of these big ideas is essential. And because some of them would yield implications directly at odds with current practice, professional leadership is absolutely vital. This leadership can derive from the positional authority of principals and their designees, but it also emerges from teacher leaders and others in the teacher corps who hold positions (department chairs, master teachers, instructional coaches, etc.) that afford them influence. The interactions with power are important; educators with formal authority can gain attention by virtue of their position, but the ideas they bring forward must make sense to all teachers. As was noted in Chapter 2, it is the ideas in a professional organization that provide the energy for action. Although formal leaders can impose their will, professional leadership organized around powerful big ideas is essential for deep change.

Brief descriptions are offered in the next section for each of the big ideas that underpin conversations about teaching. These concepts are derived from extensive research literature, from the disparate literature of cognitive psychology, organizational development, and business. Although they make sense, many of them are not consistent with the prevailing understandings and consequent practices of the educational community. Their implications for planning and implementing learning experiences are profound; observations of teaching and conversations about practice are inevitably shaped by them.

The descriptions below provide the material for an initial exploration of the concepts. But for a more in-depth appreciation of them, and their impact on practice, reading some of the material cited in the Reference section is recommended.

What Constitutes Important Learning?

The question of important learning has a few different aspects to it, which are described below:

- The skills and knowledge needed by students who will be citizens and in the workforce until the second half of the 21st century

- How school content is conceptualized and described (For example, does mathematics consist of procedures to be memorized and applied, or concepts to be understood, or some combination of the two?)

A critical examination of these two factors is necessary and will have an enormous impact on conversations about teaching. And as with others of the big ideas, consensus on them among members of a professional community is essential for discussions about teaching to have meaning.

Necessary Skills and Knowledge

As pointed out by policymakers and educators over the past several decades, today's elementary students will be active members of their communities forty years from now. If one contemplates the dramatic changes that have taken place over the past forty years, one must recognize that it would be impossible to predict, with any degree of confidence, the precise knowledge and skills that will be needed by these students. The revolution in information technology, of course, has had an incalculable impact on all aspects of people's daily and professional lives.

In addition, economic globalization has provided inescapable evidence that what was considered a good education two generations ago is now hopelessly inadequate. A community must be able to ensure an investor (e.g., an automobile manufacturer) that it can offer an educated workforce; in this sense, it is competing with other communities for that company's investment. In addition, however, jobs of all skill levels are now being shifted to other countries. American communities, then, are competing not only with neighboring communities but also towns and cities in India and China. As Thomas Friedman put it succinctly in a column in the *New York Times* on December 13, 2006, "Why should any employer anywhere in the world pay Americans to do highly skilled work—if other people, just as well educated, are available in less developed countries for half our wages?"

This economic argument is compelling: The global economy is highly integrated; very little work can't be automated and digitized and accomplished anywhere in the world. Furthermore, the United States lags behind other industrialized countries in every international assessment and measures of Internet penetration, and although achievement levels of American students are on average higher than those in India and China, those countries produce far more graduates, in sheer numbers, than does the United States. To sustain high levels of economic activity and growth, then, American schools must prepare their students for a world that is impossible to predict with any assurance but in which people will have to be adaptable and flexible so they can succeed in changing conditions. Schools were designed in the 19th century, after all, to equip their graduates to do routine work. Those are not the needs of the 21st century, with a premium on creativity and innovation. It's more than a question of a group of students being left behind, victims of poor teaching in chaotic conditions; we could have an entire generation left in the dust of the global economy.

No discussion of the skills and knowledge required of American graduates from high school would be complete without acknowledgement of the contribution to this debate of the Common Core State Standards (CCSS). Created by the Council of Chief State School Officers (CCSSO) and the National Governors Association (NGA), and promulgated in 2010, they identify the content (in literacy and mathematics) students must master in order to be "college and career ready." These new and rigorous standards, and their accompanying assessments, were adopted almost immediately by the vast majority of states.

Since 2010, the landscape around the CCSS has become much murkier, as some states create their own variations on the standards, or—in some cases—abandon them altogether. The reasons behind these political dynamics are complex and many faceted, and the future of the Common Core Standards is uncertain; however, what is well established is that today's students, in order to participate fully in the economy of the future, must be in possession of much higher levels of skill than was required in the past.

In light of this reality, consensus is emerging that our schools must graduate students with the following skills:

- Deep understanding and skill in the traditional academic disciplines, including written and oral communication (reflecting the CCSS and recent developments in other disciplines, such as science)

- International understanding
- Innovation, initiative, and creativity
- Critical thinking and problem solving
- Interpersonal skills, including collaboration and leadership
- Knowing how to learn and question

What is well established is that today's students, in order to participate fully in the economy of the future, must be in possession of much higher levels of skill than was required in the past.

The skills needed for an educated citizenry are no less demanding. Voters are asked to evaluate candidates' positions on a wide range of complex issues; their judgment requires an understanding of public policy and historical trends. One way to think about citizenship skills is to contemplate the demands of serving on a jury. As Justice Leland DeGrasse wrote in a decision in 2001,

A capable and productive citizen doesn't simply turn up for jury service. Rather, she is capable of serving impartially on trials that may require learning unfamiliar facts and concepts and new ways to communicate and reach decisions with her fellow jurors. . . . Jurors may be called on to decide complex matters that require the verbal, reasoning, math, science, and socialization skills that should be imparted in public schools. Jurors today must determine questions of fact concerning DNA evidence, statistical analyses, and convoluted financial fraud, to name only three topics.

The Description of Content

Virtually all states have adopted rigorous content standards for student learning, whether or not they are using the Common Core. The standards vary considerably in their level of detail (their grain size) and in the type of knowledge described. But regardless of how the standards are written and the verbs used to indicate student performance (identify, describe), the manner in which teachers think about the content they teach has enormous influence on their practice.

School learning comes in different forms: Some of it represents factual knowledge (knowing *that . . .*), some is procedural knowledge (knowing *how to . . .*), and some is conceptual understanding. In addition, there are skills: communication skills (for example, reading and writing), thinking skills (e.g., analyzing information, formulating and testing hypotheses), and social skills (e.g., collaborating with others, seeing another person's point of view). Last, there are values and dispositions (perseverance, open-mindedness). Clearly, all these types of learning are important, although some have traditionally been more emphasized (because they are easier to assess) in state content standards than others. In particular, factual knowledge and procedural knowledge are stressed over conceptual understanding and thinking skills. The danger is that in their zeal to prepare students for success in passing high-stakes state assessments, teachers will devote greater attention to those lower-level aspects of learning, ignoring the (more interesting and challenging) aspects of higher-level performance.

Some international assessments, notably Trends in International Math and Science Study (TIMSS) and Programme for International Student Assessment (PISA), and the National Assessment of Educational Practice (NAEP: called "the nation's report card") assess higher-level learning. This is primarily due to the fact that rather than testing every student, they conduct a sample, thereby using deeper assessments than is possible with large-scale, machine-scorable tests. It has been recognized for some time that, on these international assessments, American students don't fare nearly as well as their peers in other countries. Some have tried to explain away this phenomenon by pointing out that in this country, all students attend high school and are included in the pool of students to be sampled; while in many other countries, high school is selective and includes only the most capable and prepared. Although this may be the case for assessments of seventeen-year-olds, it can't explain the differences among nine-year-olds, where universal education prevails in every advanced country.

The differences in educational attainment are striking. "On a test of mathematics achievement, for example, the highest-scoring classroom in the US did not perform as well as the lowest-scoring classroom in the Japanese sample" (Stigler & Hiebert, 1999, p. 5). In fact, the United States' system of teaching actually reinforced attention to lower-level math skills (p. 111). The US math classrooms were characterized by "unchallenging, procedurally oriented math lessons that are unnecessarily fragmented (p. 125). Other results are less dramatic, but the patterns are clear; the academic performance of American students lags well behind that of those from other countries.

Explanations of these phenomena have varied from structural factors (the length of time students spend in school, pay and social status of teachers) to actual instructional factors. The latter appear to hold the greatest potential for improving the performance of American students. And it begins with understanding how the content to be learned is viewed in different countries and continuing with an examination of whether the American conceptualization of practice can yield optimal results in terms of high-level learning.

The most detailed study of this phenomenon was conducted by Stigler and Hiebert (2005); they focused on the teaching of mathematics and compared approaches in seven countries: the United States, Australia, Czech Republic, Hong Kong SAR, Netherlands, Switzerland, and Japan. Their approach was to analyze hundreds of videotaped lessons from the seven countries and to interview the teachers. They discovered significant differences in various aspects of practice, beginning with how teachers regard the content they teach and the assumptions on which their instruction is based.

Not only did the six other countries in the sample show higher math achievement than the United States, the teaching methods vastly differed. While math instruction in the United

States tended to focus on a "constellation of features that reinforced attention to lower-level mathematical skills" (p. 112), the other countries focused on a balance of attention to challenging curriculum and procedural learning. One of the results of the study was the comparison of the percentage of application problems in a given lesson. The United States had the lowest percentage (34%) of application problems of any of the seven countries, and Japan had the highest percentage (74%). Over double the problems in a Japanese math class were application versus the amount of routine and procedural problems being solved in US math classes. When the authors conducted an earlier study, similar results were found. In the United States, about 80 percent of concepts were just stated rather than developed, with the percentages roughly reversed for Japan. Furthermore, in US classrooms, students learned about twice as many definitions as students in the other countries. This is not to suggest that it's not important to learn definitions—it depends on what is done with them. In the United States, definitions were the beginning and end of the lesson—learning the meanings of the definitions was the point of the lesson. In contrast, the Japanese lesson taught students to use the definition to develop a proof to show, for example, that vertical angles are always equal.

These findings have profound implications. If teachers (as in the United States) believe that their mission is to help students perform mathematical procedures, their instructional strategies are very different than if they regard their role as helping students develop an understanding of complex concepts. Such a focus leads teachers to explanations followed by low-level practice, rather than a more problem-oriented approach in which students develop understanding. And because many teachers were themselves taught by teachers with an incomplete understanding of mathematical concepts, the cycle can be self-perpetuating.

The first of the big ideas, then, is for teachers to critically examine what they are teaching and to ensure that their learning outcomes do the following:

- Reflect high-level learning important to the discipline
- Represent a balance of different types of content (knowledge, skills, etc.)
- Develop conceptual understanding rather than merely facts and procedures

Once consensus on this big idea has been established, conversations about teaching can explore its implications in daily practice. For example, it is interesting to look at the work students are asked to do from the standpoint of the rigor of the content, the

The first of the big ideas, then, is for teachers to critically examine what they are teaching and to ensure that their learning outcomes do the following:

- Reflect high-level learning important to the discipline
- Represent a balance of different types of content (knowledge, skills, etc.)
- Develop conceptual understanding rather than merely facts and procedures.

extent to which it represents important conceptual learning, and whether students are challenged to develop a range of skills (e.g., collaboration and reasoning) as well as more traditional knowledge.

What Causes Learning?

Another big idea that can serve as the foundation for important professional conversations concerns the nature of learning: How is it that people learn things? How does deep conceptual understanding develop? How do individuals learn to use their minds to analyze poetry or data or evaluate the claims of competing political candidates? This question is central to the mission of schools, and it is significant that the accepted answer to it has evolved over the past several decades.

During portions of the 20th century, knowledge was equated with behavior, and therefore, learning was thought of as changing that behavior. This led to attempts to apply what had been learned from animal psychology to student learning, including stimulus-response, operant conditioning, and the creation of "teacher-proof" and completely scripted texts. Of course, a more complex view of learning had held currency previously. In 1900, in *The School and Society,* John Dewey had recognized that

> The child is already intensely active, and the question of education is the question of taking hold of his activities, of giving them direction. Through direction, through organized use, they tend toward valuable results, instead of scattering or being left to merely impulsive expression. (Dewey quoted in Dewey, 1959)

Although not all of Dewey's (1959) views are widely shared, most educators now recognize that he was essentially correct about the active nature of learning, that for students to acquire conceptual knowledge, they must engage with the ideas, they must construct their understanding. It's important to understand what this constructivist approach to learning is and what it is not. When educators argue that students must create their own understanding, it's not that the teacher cedes control over the classroom to students. Far from it; it is the teacher who decides what it is the students will learn (the learning outcomes). The constructivist position merely describes how it is that students come to learn what the teacher intends, and it appreciates the complex nature of learning.

An example from mathematics provides a vivid example of a constructivist methodology. The elementary mathematics curriculum typically includes the formulae for the area and perimeter of geometric shapes; the typical approach would be to present the formulae with probably a brief explanation of what the terms mean and to then provide opportunities for students to practice applying the formulae to calculate the areas and/or perimeters of some shapes. In a constructivist classroom, on the other hand, a teacher might present students with the following problem: "You have 64 feet of fencing. What are the measurements of the largest dog run you could construct?" To solve this problem, students would have to explore not only the formulae for area and perimeter but the relationships between the two.

In such a classroom, students would wrestle with a concrete problem and discover, no doubt, different approaches to its solution. Important learning, of course, would come in the group discussion, in which different approaches were shared and compared as to their accuracy and efficiency. In the course of the discussion, the teacher would explain (if such an explanation were needed) the formulae for area and perimeter, building on what the students had discovered. In addition, students would find that the closer the shape is to a square (if it has rigid sides) or a circle (if the fencing is permitted to bend) the larger the area for a given perimeter. This is a powerful understanding and introduces students to the concept of a variable, central to later understanding of algebra.

This is not to argue that there is never a place for rote learning. Indeed, memorization is the only way to learn, for example, French vocabulary words. But an understanding of the roots of those words can make the process of memorization both easier and more interesting. Or in elementary mathematics, students learn that every time 2 is multiplied by 6 in whichever sequence the numbers are given and in whichever representation used, the answer is always 12. Once the concept of multiplication is understood, however, the multiplication facts must simply be committed to memory.

The danger for learning occurs when teaching of facts and procedures is substituted for conceptual understanding. That is, students can simply memorize procedures for getting the right answer, or the facts of history, or the definitions of terms in science. But without the conceptual underpinning supporting their memory, it is vulnerable to being forgotten, to not being available to apply to other situations. The concepts just memorized can't in any meaningful sense be said to have been *learned*. Constructivist teaching, on the other hand, aims for conceptual, flexible, understanding with students in control of powerful understanding.

Educators have, for some time, labored under the false notion that one must master the basic before one can move on to the more interesting application of the basic knowledge. We now know that thinking and content develop together and that the thinking results in the content learning. This finding has been well documented through research. In fact, Shelagh Gallagher and William Stepien (1996) have found that research in cognitive psychology has documented the "benefits of learning in a complex environment. Instruction that fosters higher-order thinking can result in learners who can construct meaningful connections between pieces of information, transfer information to new settings . . . and are motivated to learn" (p. 53). Indeed, Lauren Resnick and Leopold Klopfer (1989) argue that "one of the most significant ideas emerging from recent research on thinking is that the mental processes we have customarily associated with thinking are not restricted to some advanced or 'higher order' stage of mental development. Instead, 'thinking skills' are intimately involved in successful learning of even elementary levels of reading, mathematics, and other subjects" (p. 1).

The most significant research finding is deceptively simple: Learning is done *by the learner.* That is, as teachers we tend to think that our students learn on account of what we do. But that is a mistake: Our students don't learn because of what *we* do; they learn because of what *they* do. Our challenge, then, is to design learning experiences for students that are interesting and that yield the learning we desire. Some educators make extensive use of physical (manipulative) materials in their classrooms. Indeed, a physical representation can aid in student acquisition of some concepts, particularly in elementary mathematics. But they are no panacea: Students can be as mindless in their work with manipulatives as they are with a worksheet. The larger point is that school is, for students, more than hands-on; it is minds-on. For students, school is not a spectator sport.

> Our students don't learn because of what *we* do; they learn because of what *they* do.

The second big idea, then, refers to how students learn. For them to acquire important concepts and skills, students must be

- mentally active, making connections, formulating hypotheses;
- linking new understanding to what is known;
- participating in in-depth, structured reflection; and
- engaging in collaboration.

The nature of learning provides rich opportunities for conversations about teaching and how the principles of learning are reflected daily in classroom practice. Observers of classrooms can be alert to the nature of student engagement and the extent to which students have opportunities to develop understanding based on intellectual activity. These observations can then provide the foundation for important conversations among educators.

How Are Students Motivated?

Yet another important big idea that provides the raw material for powerful professional conversations concerns how students are motivated to work hard. Important learning, after all, requires commitment and perseverance on the part of students: What convinces them to expend the effort? Understanding recent research and the implications of that research for teaching are critical to strengthening teaching practice; as with other aspects of practice, strengthening is enhanced through professional conversation.

Every teacher holds a mental image of interested, motivated students who engage willingly with challenging content, who behave respectfully, and who complete their work with commitment and energy. The reality for many teachers is, unfortunately, somewhat at odds with this vision: Their students are sullen, alienated, and appear to be looking for ways to bend the rules to their advantage. Even young children, although they will usually comply with the school's ways of doing things, many are devoid of the energy in class that is so apparent on the playground or at home after school and on the weekends.

The second big idea, then, refers to how students learn. For them to acquire important concepts and skills, students must be

- mentally active, making connections, formulating hypotheses;
- linking new understanding to what is known;
- participating in in-depth, structured reflection; and
- engaging in collaboration.

And yet there are some teachers who do seem to enlist students' best efforts, where they become engaged in complex projects, doing difficult work. There is a palpable energy in these classes; an observer can feel it when walking in the door. What, one might ask, are those teachers' secrets? Are their classrooms run on fear ("Don't smile before Christmas"), or are they permissive? How do they do it? More than likely, they have heeded William Glasser's (1986) words: "All living creatures, and we are no exception, only do what they believe is most satisfying to them, and the main reason our schools are less effective than we would like them to be is that, where students are concerned, we have failed to appreciate this fact" (p. 8).

It's important to remember the four-year-olds everyone has known. No one has to cajole them to learn new things; they are eager in their pursuit of new experiences and new knowledge. Young children appear driven to figure things out, and in fact, one of the biggest challenges of parenting is to prevent them from harming themselves from dangers they don't understand. However, by the time these same children leave elementary school, many of them are lethargic and seem to have lost their curiosity. So what has happened in the intervening years? Have the schools themselves somehow drained children of their natural inclinations toward learning? And how can we explain older students' pursuit of difficult new skills, for example, riding a skateboard, even in the face of repeated falls? What makes them persevere?

A critical distinction when considering human motivation is the one between intrinsic and extrinsic motivation: Intrinsic motivation is that which is driven from within an individual, whereas extrinsic motivation is imposed from the outside. The external reward may be anything valued, including recognition from a parent or teacher. Children playing in a stream pursue it because they are intrinsically motivated; those who work on a project to get a good grade are extrinsically motivated. Each has its place, of course. Many important things, such as state capitals, would not be learned if students were not influenced by extrinsic factors.

However, the situation is complex. Many studies have confirmed that extrinsic motivation tends to drive out intrinsic factors. Edward Deci (1995, pp. 25–26) reports experiments with graduate students who were given a puzzle to solve—they found it interesting and were intrinsically motivated to work on it. Then, two groups of students were given the puzzle: One group was paid to solve it; the other group not. Then, when the experiment was (supposedly) finished the students were told to wait for a few minutes while the leader went out of the room to do some paperwork. Those who had been paid for their participation chose not to continue playing with the puzzle, while those who had not been paid did. That is, being paid appears to have destroyed what intrinsic motivation had been there previously. Many other studies have reached similar conclusions. Thomas Sergiovanni (1992, p. 24) cites the well-known David Greene and Mark Lepper (1974) study with young children and felt-tip markers. Once they were offered a reward, they were much less interested in playing with them. The issue for schools is not whether we should banish extrinsic motivation; that would be impossible and probably undesirable. But many schools, as organizations, rely exclusively on extrinsic motivation and have ignored the research on intrinsic motivation. This is an omission with a high cost; for many students, school, rather than a place for interesting exploration of important learning, has become a setting for unrelieved boredom and drudgery. And most teachers, because they are not familiar with the principles of intrinsic motivation, are not able to take advantage of findings with highly relevant and powerful implications for daily practice.

So what is known about intrinsic motivation? What principles should we incorporate into day-to-day teaching to capture students' best energies? There is considerable consensus on the major research findings, extending over many decades. The first is the primacy of basic physical needs in influencing behavior; if people don't have at least adequate food, shelter, and warmth, all their energies must be devoted to acquiring those. This explains the importance of breakfast and lunch programs for children from poor backgrounds; if they are hungry they can't begin to focus on what is being done in school.

But beyond the basic physical imperatives, all human beings are motivated by powerful psychological needs. These have been identified and described by Glasser (2001), Deci (1995), and Robert White (1959) among others. They are summarized below.

- *Belonging and making connections with others.* Human beings are social creatures and must make connections with others. Students will frequently perform their best work when they know it is to be presented to the class—they care deeply about the opinions of their peers. Furthermore, students find working with classmates to be far more engaging than individual effort, to which many teachers who make use of student group work can attest.

- *Competence or mastery.* Understanding difficult content, like mastery in any field, is enormously satisfying. Part of the satisfaction is the struggle itself: If it's too easy, if there is no challenge, the result is cheapened. Mastery of complex content, then, represents *power*.

- *Autonomy or freedom.* Of course, students in school can't have unlimited choices; teachers must make essential decisions regarding what is to be learned and what students are to do. However, students are highly sensitive to practices that appear to reflect a teacher's unreasonable and arbitrary use of power, and when students can select work (from among a selection of acceptable options) they are more inclined to make a commitment to it.

- *Intellectual challenge.* Inquiry-based learning acknowledges that students' curiosity is a powerful motivator, to the extent that learning tasks invite students to solve a problem, or resolve incongruous events, or understand anomalies; students are driven by an innate curiosity to resolve the discrepancy.

It's important to recognize that teachers are subject to the same motivational factors as their students. Teachers, too, prefer collaboration to isolation in their work, and the social structures in a school (such as doughnuts on Fridays) contribute to a sense of cohesion among members of a faculty. Similarly, teachers resist overly controlling environments and are highly motivated by the need to feel competent and masterful in their work. Finally, solving problems related to their practice is highly rewarding; deciding on a course of action to solve a complex problem is far preferable to following someone else's script.

As for students, many of the discipline problems teachers must handle or that turn up at the principal's office are a direct consequence of students' needs not being met. The class clown may receive sufficient recognition from other students to make the disciplinary consequences of his behavior worth it to him; another student may prefer being sent to the office over having her ignorance revealed in class. It's an interesting and revealing exercise to analyze common discipline problems in light of motivational theory. Teachers frequently discover that their students' behavior problems are quite purposeful from a motivational point of view.

The third big idea, then, concerns student motivation and suggests that students will bring energy and commitment to their work when they have opportunities for

- purposeful and respectful interactions with other students;
- the development of competence and mastery in important content;
- a measure of autonomy and control over how they spend their time (this is usually provided through choice in activities); and
- solving interesting problems and challenges, addressing puzzlements.

The third big idea concerns student motivation and suggests students need

- purposeful and respectful interactions,
- development of competence and mastery in content,
- some autonomy and control of time, and
- to be challenged by interesting problems.

An exploration of student motivation through conversations about teaching provides opportunities for educators to delve into how teachers help students develop the resilience they need to take on difficult intellectual challenges. These conversations built on actual classroom events enable the discussions to deepen the understanding of everyone participating.

What Is Intelligence, and How Do Students' Views Influence Their Actions?

The last big idea and one that contributes to the ways in which educators view the others, concerns the nature of intelligence, and why the perceptions of both students and teachers are important. Professional conversations frequently reveal differences in how different educators regard intelligence (whether it is a fixed commodity, for example, or whether it can be developed); such differences have large implications for classroom practice.

Important research has focused on different ways in which both students and teachers view intelligence; recent findings indicate that these beliefs have a powerful impact on students' willingness to work hard and their academic success. This research has been described by, among others, Carol Dweck (2000), a social psychologist at Stanford University. She has conducted a series of important studies investigating the different attitudes students (and their teachers) hold about intelligence, and why it's important.

The foundation of Dweck's (2000) work has been her identification of two fundamentally different views of intelligence: fixed and malleable. Those with a fixed view of intelligence regard it as something one is born with, the hand one has been dealt. There is not much a person can do about how smart a person is, in this view. On the other hand, some people hold a view of intelligence profoundly different: In the malleable view of intelligence, smart is not something you *are* but something you *become* through application and hard work. When a student says, "I'm just not good at math," he or she is reflecting a fixed view of intelligence.

The consequences for students of these different views of intelligence are profound. The first deals with students' willingness to work hard. Students with a fixed view of their intelligence seek validation of their self-concept through success in school tasks. They tend to avoid activities that might challenge this view; therefore, when confronted with a choice between an easy task and a more difficult one, they will select the easy task. Students with a malleable view of their intelligence, on the other hand, tend to prefer challenging tasks; they see them as more fun. Furthermore, and paradoxically, students with a fixed view of intelligence are unwilling to work hard or be seen to be working hard. Their reasoning is particularly revealing. "If I were really smart, I wouldn't have to work hard at this. In fact, if I have to work hard, it must mean that I am not very smart."

The second, and in some ways even more important consequence of different views of intelligence concerns students' responses when they encounter the inevitable difficulties in learning complex material. Those with a fixed view of their intelligence become helpless, in effect giving up. Students with a malleable view of intelligence, on the other hand, are far more resilient; when they encounter difficulty, they take it as a challenge to be overcome. Dweck (2000) calls the response of these students to difficulties mastery oriented.

Dweck (2000) is careful to point out that people who hold a malleable view of intelligence don't deny that there are differences among individuals in how much they know at any given time or how quickly they can master new material. "It's just that they focus on the idea that everyone, with effort and guidance, can increase their intellectual abilities" (p. 3).

The implications for students of these different views are enormous. In an important study, Dweck (2006), in her research with colleagues, measured students' mindsets as they made the transition to junior high school—did they believe their intelligence was a fixed trait or something they could develop? They then followed them for the next two years. For many students, the transition to junior high school is hard (the environment is less personalized, their grades go down, etc.). But in their sample, only those students with a fixed mindset had those difficulties—the students' grades with the growth mindset actually went up. "In the fixed mindset, adolescence is one big test. 'Am I smart or dumb? Am I good-looking or ugly? Am I cool or nerdy? Am I a winner or a loser?' . . . It's no wonder that many adolescents mobilize their resources, not for learning, but to protect their egos. And one of the main ways they do this . . . is by not trying" (p. 58).

Because of these implications, it's important for the adults (parents and teachers) in children's lives to help them cultivate a malleable view of intelligence. Paradoxically, praising students for their intelligence is counterproductive. Dweck (2006) summarizes her research succinctly.

> After seven experiments with hundreds of children, we had some of the clearest findings I've ever seen: Praising children's intelligence harms their motivation and it harms their performance. How can that be? Don't children love to be praised? Yes, children love praise. And they especially love to be praised for their intelligence and their talent. It really does give them a boost, a special glow—but only for the moment. The minute they hit a snag, their confidence goes out the window and their motivation hits rock bottom. If success means they're smart, the failure means they're dumb. That's the fixed mindset. (p. 170)

And she follows with this observation: "When we say to children, 'Wow, you did that so quickly!' or 'Look, you didn't make any mistakes!' what message are we sending? We are telling them that what we prize are speed and perfection. Speed and perfection are the enemy of difficult learning" (Dweck, 2006, p. 173). Instead of praising intelligence, Dweck suggests, teachers should praise perseverance and strategy: "You have tried lots of different methods to solve this problem, and it looks like you have done it!" (p. 173).

Haim Ginnott (1969), during his life's work with children, came to a similar conclusion. "Praise should deal, not with the child's personality attributes, but with his efforts and achievements" (p. 57). And Alfie Kohn (1993) has concluded that praise can undermine children's intrinsic motivation. When children are praised, he argues, the praise, rather than the work itself, becomes the motivation for future effort.

The fourth big idea addresses the impact of different views of intelligence, the impact of these different concepts on student commitment to hard work, and their resilience when confronted with challenges in learning. The classroom implications of these findings suggest the following:

- Students are well served by the acquisition of a malleable view of intelligence.
- Teachers (and parents) can assist in students' development of such a view and of healthy attitudes about their own power in shaping their learning by praising student perseverance and use of strategy in their learning.

The fourth big idea addresses the impact of different views of intelligence, the impact of these different concepts on student commitment to hard work, and their resilience when confronted with challenges in learning.

- Students are well served by the acquisition of a malleable view of intelligence.
- Teachers (and parents) can assist in students' development of such a view and of healthy attitudes about their own power in shaping their learning.

Students' and teachers' views of intelligence are reflected constantly in interactions in the classroom; observations of classroom events can supply rich raw material for conversations about this important area of practice. In particular, in their professional conversations, educators can explore the ways in which teachers encourage students' effort and learning strategies and how they convince students to persevere even in the face of temporary setbacks.

The Merging of All These Ideas

These big ideas offer an important vision for education, a vision that is at odds with prevailing practice in many schools. They serve as the foundation for conversations between teachers and administrators, and among teachers. They also serve as the important ideas around which educational leaders (both teachers and administrators), working together, must develop understanding that results in action.

The concepts described in this chapter reinforce one another and have essential implications for practice. In essence, they all suggest that educators must heed this research when they design learning experiences for students that engage them actively in developing conceptual understanding. The consequences of this shift in thinking are profound: Although educators and researchers have tended to describe teaching in terms of the tasks of teaching as in, for example, *Enhancing Professional Practice: A Framework for Teaching* (Danielson, 2007), we must shift our focus to school as an experience *for students.*

The merging of these big ideas about student learning and motivation, about the nature of intelligence, and about what is worth learning provide much material for important conversations among educators. These conversations get at the heart of what is important for schools to incorporate into their practices, but until there is professional consensus about them, each individual is likely to be working alone, in isolation from colleagues.

The big ideas suggest the following implications, any of which provides a great foundation for meaningful conversations between teachers and administrators and between other teachers:

- What is the teacher's purpose in any learning activity? Does that purpose reflect important learning and a view of content as conceptual understanding as well as the learning of facts and procedures?

- What are the students actually doing? What is the level of intellectual rigor? What choices do they have? What are their opportunities for reflection and closure on their learning?

- To what extent has the teacher succeeded in creating a learning community in the class? To what degree do students assume responsibility for their learning?

Summary

Professional conversations in schools take place, as was noted in Chapter 2, within the web of relationships among teachers and administrators; those relationships are influenced by the varying degrees of power and positional authority wielded by different individuals. To yield educational practices that result in high levels of student learning, however, the professional interactions among individuals in the school must be governed by powerful big ideas that reflect learning and, indeed, what is worth learning in the 21st century.

A critical application of positional authority, then, is to forge consensus, among all members of a school's faculty, on the big ideas described in this chapter. These concepts provide the foundation for how teachers design learning experiences for students and the specific topics for ongoing dialogue. The specific implications of these big ideas and suggestions for engaging in important professional conversations are the subjects of the following chapters.

4 → The Topics for Conversations

Professional conversation is unparalleled in its potential for stimulating in-depth reflection and deep learning on the part of teachers. This phenomenon—the power of conversation to serve as a catalyst for profound insights—has been recognized for some time. But what should the conversations be about? One option is to discuss theoretical matters, and indeed, such conversations can be extremely interesting and productive. But another option is to build professional conversations on the events of an observed class; these are the types of conversations described in this book. Even a brief classroom visit (5–10 minutes) can yield sufficient information on which to structure a productive conversation, and the conversation will have ready reference to actual events in the classroom which both parties to the conversation have witnessed.

In the conduct of professional conversations, it is important to determine the appropriate stance for an observer (a principal, supervisor, or instructional coach) to adopt. To what extent should the observer set the agenda and manage the path of the conversation? Does the observer take the lead, or is it a matter for the teacher to determine?

In a pure coaching conversation, when teachers invite another educator (colleague, instructional coach, supervisor, or administrator) to provide another set of eyes for an issue they are addressing, it is appropriate, even necessary, for the teachers themselves to establish the purpose of the observation and the type of information sought. For example, a teacher might suspect that he is directing more challenging questions to the boys or inviting participation during a class discussion from only one half of the room. In a coaching conversation, the teacher requesting the feedback determines what information the observer should be collecting about the class.

But another important type of conversation, and the focus of this book, is the conversation following an informal, frequently brief, observation in a teacher's classroom. The observer is typically an instructional coach, a supervisor, or an administrator, an individual whose own responsibilities permit the opportunity for informal visits to classrooms. Most teachers, after all, have full teaching loads with very little time to spend in other teachers' classrooms; thus, the vast majority of the informal professional conversations described in this book will occur between teachers and someone in a formal leadership (although not necessarily supervisory) capacity.

Power, Leadership, and the Big Ideas

The topics for conversation described in this chapter are derived directly from the big ideas outlined in Chapter 3. In that discussion, important concepts, underlying content, student learning and motivation, and the nature of intelligence were presented with their implications for classroom practice. But some of these implications are, themselves, overlapping; hence, when an instructional coach, supervisor, or administrator stops into a classroom, it's important to have a clear sense of what one might be able to see there that would reflect the big ideas.

Furthermore, if formal school leaders, typically site administrators, have followed the advice of this book (presented in detail in Chapter 8) and have forged consensus on the big ideas underlying practice, there is transparency in what a visitor could expect to observe in a classroom. That is, if everyone in a school accepts that students learn through their own intellectual engagement with content (asking questions, making connections, analyzing information, etc.), then an observer would expect to see students engaged in such activities. When consensus on such big ideas has been established, then it is understood that the implications of such ideas are always on the table for discussion; initiating a conversation on the intellectual rigor, for example, of an activity, does not constitute a "gotcha" by an administrator. Rather, it simply reflects the faculty's consensus on the big ideas about learning that are the centerpiece of all professional conversation and that an important component of student engagement is intellectual rigor. Furthermore, because such ideas are complex, the conversations are not a matter of finding fault, or even providing feedback, on what a teacher is doing; rather, they are professional conversations about how an activity might have been more rigorous or might have engaged students in more high-order thinking than what was observed. It is *professional* conversation, among colleagues, even when one has greater formal power than the other.

So what are the topics (or several in combination), derived from the big ideas, that could serve as the basis for a meaningful conversation following even a brief observation? They are listed below:

- Clarity of instructional purpose and accuracy of content

- Safe, respectful, supportive and challenging learning environment

- Classroom management

- Student intellectual engagement

- Successful learning of all students

- Professionalism

Educators familiar with the framework for teaching (Danielson, 2007) will notice considerable overlap between the framework and the topics for conversation presented here. Indeed, the components described in the framework comprise the heart of teaching, much of which may be observed in the classroom. They provide a finely grained set of competencies for observation. And as described in *Enhancing Professional Practice: A Framework for Teaching* (Danielson, 2007), the domains and components of teaching rest on fundamental assumptions about learning and motivation that form the heart of the clusters presented here.

However, for the purposes of informal conversations about practice, and for coaching and learning conversations, it is preferable to use a "grain size" larger than that offered in the framework for teaching. When making a brief, informal observation, it's difficult for a coach or supervisor to hold a large number of discrete components of teaching in mind; fewer, bigger concepts are more useful. Even for a formal observation of teaching, the larger clusters can be helpful, enabling the observer to focus on the larger threads of practice.

The *Six Clusters* is a description of the skills demonstrated by accomplished teachers in promoting high levels of student performance—skills based on foundational knowledge and dispositions and grounded in a deep understanding of the nature of human learning. The clusters are an outgrowth of *The Framework for Teaching* (the FfT), which has been validated through empirical studies as predictive of student learning as measured by state assessments. But while the FfT has enjoyed wide acceptance among members of the professional community of educators, its level of detail also makes it cumbersome for everyday use. The clusters are an attempt to distill the big ideas of the FfT's four domains and twenty-two components

The *Six Clusters* is a description of the skills demonstrated by accomplished teachers in promoting high levels of student performance—skills based on foundational knowledge and dispositions and grounded in a deep understanding of the nature of human learning.

into an efficient tool (composed of six large concepts) that can serve as the focus not only for evaluation, but for professional growth by teachers through not only their own reflection on practice but also their conversations with colleagues, mentors and coaches, and supervisors.

The clusters—like the full framework—are themselves generic in nature; that is, they apply to all teaching situations, in all disciplines, and at different ages and levels. Furthermore, they reflect teaching to high standards of student learning, as reflected in the Common Core State Standards and other high-level standards. Some of these principles of teaching for CCSS learning are, indeed, generic. For example, teaching for deep conceptual understanding, the use of precise academic language, and the skills of argumentation are evident in all disciplines. Similarly, student skill in questioning the reasoning of classmates and persevering in challenging content occur in all settings.

On the other hand, teaching occurs in real settings, with real students, and about specific content. Therefore, while there is a generic skill of argumentation, for example, it plays out differently in mathematics than in literacy. Hence, the clusters document is offered in several versions: a generic version, a literacy version, and a mathematics version. Furthermore, literacy skills are evident not only in English classrooms for literary analysis, but also for reading for meaning in other disciplines, such as social studies and science. These versions translate the generic language of the narratives and critical attributes, where appropriate, into content-specific language to guide both teachers and leaders.

Furthermore, while the clusters—like the full Framework for Teaching—reflects teaching practices that are common across all settings, actual teaching occurs with students in all their diversity—cultural, linguistic, and developmental. Hence, accomplished teachers must be familiar with their students' individual characteristics and needs and create their plans and provide instruction accordingly. Therefore, when the language of the framework refers to attending to individual students, it is to this full range of learners that it applies. These are the "common themes" of the framework for teaching, which are infused in all of the components, and elements, and ensure an inclusive environment for learning.

For those familiar with *The Framework for Teaching,* the following table summarizes the relationship between the clusters and the full FfT, together with the ways in which teachers demonstrate their skill for each one.

Table 4.1 provides a cross-reference of the topics presented in this chapter and the components of the framework for teaching.

Table 4.1 The Link Between the Six Large Component Clusters and the Full Framework for Teaching

Cluster	FfT Components/ Elements	Sources of Evidence
1. Clarity of Instructional Purpose and Accuracy of Content *To what extent does the teacher demonstrate depth of important content knowledge and conduct the class with a clear and ambitious purpose, reflective of the standards for the discipline and appropriate to the students' levels of knowledge and skill?* *To what degree are the elements of a lesson (the sequence of topics, instructional strategies, and materials and resources) well designed and executed and aligned with the purposes of the lesson? To what extent are they designed to engage students in high-level learning in the discipline?*	• 1a, 1b, 1c, 1d: Knowledge of content, clarity, and appropriateness for students of instructional outcomes; resources for classroom use • 1e: Planned activities aligned to instructional purpose • 3a: Expectations for learning, accuracy of content, clarity of explanations, use of academic language • 3b, 3c: Questions, activities, and assignments aligned to instructional purpose	• Instructional purpose, planned instructional activities on written document • Observation • Statements to students about purpose, conversation with students • Accuracy of content • Alignment of questions, activities, and assignments to purpose • Reflection: Success in achieving the lesson objectives?

2. Safe, Respectful, Supportive, and Challenging Learning Environment
 	
To what extent do the interactions between teacher and students, and among students, demonstrate genuine caring and a safe, respectful, supportive, and
	• 2a: All
	• 2b: Expectations for learning and achievement, student perseverance in challenging work, and pride in that work
		• Observation:
		  ○ Interactions of students and teacher
		  ○ Student perseverance and pride
		• Student surveys?

(Continued)

Table 4.1 (Continued)

Cluster	FfT Components/ Elements	Sources of Evidence
also challenging learning environment? Do teachers convey high expectations for student learning and encourage hard work and perseverance? Is the environment safe for risk taking? Do students take pride in their work and demonstrate a commitment to mastering challenging content?		

3. Classroom Management
 	
Is the classroom well run and organized? Are classroom routines and procedures clear and carried out efficiently by both teacher and students with little loss of instructional time? To what extent do students themselves take an active role in their smooth operation? Are directions for activities clearly explained so that there is no confusion? Do students not only understand and comply with standards of conduct but also play an active part in setting the tone for maintaining those standards? How does the physical environment support the learning activities?
	• 2c: All
	• 2d: All
	• 2e: All
		• Observation:
		  o routines
		  o student conduct
		  o physical environment, etc.

4. Student Intellectual Engagement *To what extent are students intellectually engaged in a*	• 1e: Design of instruction • 2b: Importance of the content	• Planning documents • Observation: o The nature of the work students are doing

Cluster	FfT Components/ Elements	Sources of Evidence
classroom of high intellectual energy? What is the nature of what students are doing? Are they being challenged to think and make connections through both the instructional activities and the questions explored? Do the teacher's explanations of content correctly model academic language and invite intellectual work by students? Are students asked to explain their thinking, constructing logical arguments citing evidence, and to question the thinking of others? Are the instructional strategies used by the teacher suitable to the discipline, and to what extent do they promote student agency in the learning of challenging content?	• 3a: Explanations of content: Their rigor and invitations for thinking • 3b: Quality of questions and discussions, student discourse • 3c: Intellectual challenge	○ The quality of teacher presentation of content ○ The nature of student discourse and class discussion • (If available) the worksheet or activity students are doing • (If available) samples of student work

5. Successful Learning by All Students
 	
To what extent does the teacher ensure the learning by all students? Does the teacher monitor student understanding through specifically designed questions or instructional techniques (such as exit tickets)? To what extent do students monitor their own learning and provide respectful feedback to classmates? Does the teacher make modifications
	• 1b: Knowledge of students
	• 1d: Resources for students
	• 1f: Design of summative and formative assessments aligned to outcomes
	• 3d: Monitoring of student learning, feedback to students, student self-assessment
		• Planning documents for formative and summative assessments
		• Observation:
		  ○ monitoring,
		  ○ feedback,
		  ○ adjustment
		• Reflection: Comments on learning of individuals
		• Artifacts documenting both record keeping and communication with families

(Continued)

Table 4.1 (Continued)

Cluster	FfT Components/ Elements	Sources of Evidence
in presentations or learning activities where necessary, taking into account the degree of student learning? Has he or she sought out other resources (including parents) to support students' learning? In reflection, is the teacher aware of the success of the lesson in reaching students?	• 3e: Persistence, lesson adjustment • 4a: All • 4b: All • 4c: All	
6. Professionalism *To what extent does the teacher engage with the professional community (within the school and beyond) and demonstrate a commitment to ongoing professional learning? Does the teacher collaborate productively with colleagues and contribute to the life of the school? Does the teacher engage in professional learning, and take a leadership role in the school to promote the welfare of students?*	• 1d: Resources to extend professional knowledge • 4d: All • 4e: All • 4f: All	• Artifacts documenting contributions to a professional culture, to professional learning, and to other professional activities

Primarily, the events of a lesson provide both the teacher and the observer with the raw material for analysis, permitting them to discuss events, discover patterns, and interpret student responses. Teaching skill may always be discussed in the abstract, but actual events and actual learning experiences provide exemplars of practice. The events of the lesson offer illustrations of the big ideas at work, for example, students being motivated by the opportunity for choice in their investigations or student understanding enhanced through intellectual engagement in learning. By discussing these events, teachers consolidate and extend their understanding of the ideas and are able to incorporate them increasingly into their practice.

The following sections describe the topics that can be used to inform brief classroom observations and to structure the conversations that follow.

Cluster 1: Clarity of Instructional Purpose and Accuracy of Content

Teaching is a purposeful activity; it is goal directed and designed to achieve certain well-defined ends. Even when operating within the confines of an established curriculum (as virtually all teachers are), teachers must determine the purposes for a given class on a given day. In all disciplines, those daily purposes are embedded in larger goals, which develop over time. That is, important understanding of complex concepts (such as the distinction between democratic and republican forms of government, or the behavior of prime numbers) and the skills of constructing paths of reasoning, do not lend themselves to a single day's lesson, and are not "ticked off" as complete. They develop slowly, with the purpose for a given day embedded in a longer sequence of lessons. In fact, the very phrase *habits of mind* suggests that it takes time to develop such understanding and skill and increased sophistication in content. Therefore, while it is essential for teachers to be able to demonstrate clarity of instructional purpose, those purposes are not of the type that can be considered "finished."

Clarity of instructional purpose is essential to good teaching; classroom time is, after all, limited, and available time must be used wisely. Instructional purposes are statements, then, of what the teacher intends for students to learn; they should be clear and appropriately challenging for the students in the class. It is not sufficient for a teacher to state what the students will *do* during a lesson; he or she should also be clear about what they will *learn*. Admittedly, the learning outcomes are realized for students through the tasks and investigations in which they engage, but these activities and tasks must be designed such that they serve the teacher's instructional purpose.

Clarity of purpose implies alignment with the state or district's curriculum outcomes (the Common Core State Standards or other high-level state standards), consisting of the factual, conceptual, and procedural knowledge, skills, and understandings identified in the standards. The content should be challenging and rigorous, and also appropriate for the students in the class; this idea suggests that learning outcomes may have to be differentiated to some degree to accommodate different students' backgrounds in prerequisite understanding, language proficiency, and special needs.

> It is not sufficient for a teacher to state what the students will *do* during a lesson; he or she should also be clear about what they will *learn*.

Such clarity of purpose requires deep knowledge of the content, of subject-specific pedagogy, and of one's students. Deep knowledge of content (as distinct from superficial familiarity) includes the teacher's understanding of the big ideas of the subject and of how these are related to other important concepts, both within the discipline and in other disciplines. Clarity of purpose also implies knowledge of essential prerequisite understanding, flexibility of thinking, and recognition that there are many pathways to understanding. In planning a lesson, a teacher should be clear about those pathways: what sequence of activities and tasks will lead to student understanding. It is not sufficient that an activity be fun; it must also serve an important instructional goal.

Teachers demonstrate their deep knowledge of content and pedagogy in many ways: both in planning documents and in the course of a lesson, in which the presentation of content and responses to student questions and comments are essential to learning. Indeed, a knowledgeable teacher will know whether a student's question is important to the discipline and therefore worth pursuing in depth, or whether it represents a sidebar and can be handled efficiently.

A lesson's activities, as revealed both in the planning documents and in their execution in the classroom, must serve to achieve the lesson's purpose. In a well-designed lesson, these tasks and activities are sequenced and are designed to engage students in the intellectual work of learning. Furthermore, "clarity" extends to the activity itself. Students should not be in the dark about how to complete an activity, what steps they should take, and whether it's to be done on their own or with classmates.

Well-run classrooms are purposeful and businesslike; they may be joyful, but students and teachers are clear not only about what they are doing, but also about what desired learning is being pursued. There is a sense, conveyed through both words and actions, that what's going on in the lesson is important and that learning is exhilarating and empowering. Serendipity may permit the extension of the learning into other areas, but the fundamentals are clear and are grounded in the teacher's deep knowledge of the content and of the ways to engage students in that content.

When planning to conduct conversations with teachers, in some respects the first aspect of teaching that can be addressed, if it has not been addressed previously, relates to its clarity of purpose; that is, what is it that the students are *learning?* At least, what is the teacher's intent?

> Clarity of purpose requires deep knowledge of the content, of subject-specific pedagogy, and of one's students.

When either a teacher or a supervisor observes a class in action, the instructional purpose should be clear. This may have been announced to the students at the outset, although, of course, if the observer was not present at the beginning of the lesson he or she will not have heard it. But even if the teacher has not announced directly to the class what the purpose of the lesson is or if the observer has not heard that announcement, it is essential that the teacher have a clear purpose and be able to explain it to the observer following the lesson. That is, it is not sufficient for a teacher to be clear about what the students will *do;* he or she should also be clear about what they will *learn.*

Alternatively, the teacher may not inform the students directly about the purpose of the lesson, allowing it to emerge during the lesson itself. As described more fully in Chapter 3, "The Big Ideas That Shape Professional Conversations," the students may be engaged in an activity designed to enable them to acquire the concept of pi through their own investigation. The teacher might have asked them to measure the circumference and the diameter of a number of circular objects and to analyze the data for patterns. It will be only toward the conclusion of the activity, when results of the analysis are shared among students, that the teacher will bring closure and explain to students that the constant relationship (of a little greater than 3) they have found between the circumference and diameter of all circular objects is called *pi.*

This suggests that although a visitor might ask students what they are learning, at the outset of an inquiry lesson the students might not know. However, they should be absolutely clear about their task, that is, what they are doing. And most assuredly, by the time the students have completed their investigations, they will know that the purpose of the learning activity was to build an understanding of the concept of pi.

Professional conversations offer a rich opportunity for teachers and observers to understand a lesson's purpose. As with the other topics for conversation described in this chapter, inquiring about it does not suggest that a teacher's thinking on the subject is deficient; rather, it is that every lesson should demonstrate clarity of purpose as reflected in student activities, the interactions between teacher and students, the materials being used, and the pacing of the lesson. Furthermore, teachers should be able to describe how the purpose of today's lesson relates to yesterday's lesson and what is planned for tomorrow.

When observing in a classroom, then, and initiating a professional conversation, the questions one would seek to explore related to clarity of purpose could include the following:

- What do you intend for students to learn from the lesson?
- How will you know (if you don't know now) that students did in fact learn what you intended?
- How does this learning follow from what they, and you, did yesterday and where will it lead in future lessons?
- How will you help students consolidate their understanding?
- Questions about specific observed events related to clarity of purpose

Cluster 2: Safe, Respectful, Supportive, and Challenging Learning Environment

In order to do their best work, in order to make a commitment to the activity we call school, students must feel respected and honored *as people.* They must sense that their teachers believe in their capabilities; many adults can trace their success in school, and later in their life, to a teacher who believed they could *be* somebody. For some students, this teacher may be the first, or the only, adult who has conveyed such confidence. It can be life altering.

Teachers convey their respect for students through myriad verbal and nonverbal cues, listening carefully to students' ideas, asking for clarification and elaboration, displaying sensitivity to students' feelings. A teacher's attitude may be outwardly friendly or stern, but beneath even a stern demeanor a teacher conveys an essential *caring,* a sense that each student, regardless of background or family income, is important and has potential. Thus, students need not fear that they will be belittled by the teacher or demeaned in front of other students.

The atmosphere of support and respect is not confined to students as people but extends to them as learners. Many adults are convinced that they "can't do science" or "were never good at reading poetry." While it's difficult to know the origin of such sentiments, they should never be conveyed by teachers themselves. Thus, when teachers indicate that they sincerely honor all students in their journey for understanding, then students can engage in that quest assured of deep support by the teacher. It's a safe environment, in other words, for students to take intellectual risks, to try out ideas, to question the teacher's—or the book's, or another student's—account. Students know they need not fear ridicule, or unkind sarcasm, from the teacher or from other students.

But it's not sufficient for students to feel safe from the teacher and other students in order for them to do their best work; they must also feel challenged, and they must be willing to rise to that challenge. This is partly a matter of the nature of the work itself; that work must be rigorous, engaging, and meaningful. But, in addition, students must be willing to make a commitment to it. There must be, in other words, a prevailing norm of student commitment to high-level work; those who engage in such work must not be regarded by their classmates as *geeks,* or *nerds,* or some other term that, in student culture, denotes "uncool." Furthermore, just as a classroom culture should honor intellectual work, that same culture should insist that students persevere in challenging content, sticking with it until they get it and have achieved a higher level of understanding.

Student cultural attitudes toward work vary profoundly from one age group, and from one school, to another. Overwhelmingly, young children are keen to learn and to explore the world; if

In order to do their best work, in order to make a commitment to the activity we call school, students must feel respected and honored *as people.*

instructional tasks are interesting, they will participate willingly and aim to excel. With older students, the situation is more complex; most of the efforts these students must make to succeed in school, after all, take place in private—for example, completing their homework assignments and studying for tests. But other actions occur in public, in front of their peers, such as participating in class discussions and engaging in group work. Thus, students who decide to make a commitment to high-level work in

> It's not sufficient for students to feel safe from the teacher and other students in order for them to do their best work; they must also feel challenged, and they must be willing to rise to that challenge.

school are making a public declaration of that commitment. It's essential that they not become isolated or "punished" by their peers for that commitment.

In some settings, student norms already expect such commitment, for example, schools in communities whose families appreciate the importance of a rigorous education to ensure a successful future, or schools that have made a serious commitment to creating a culture for learning. But in other settings, particularly schools serving students of poorly educated families, the challenge for educators is far greater. Students' parents may themselves not appreciate the benefits that accrue from a solid education and from further study beyond secondary school.

As D. Bruce Jackson (2003) has written so eloquently,

> Ultimately, students are in charge of how they spend their time, how they wish to be seen, who they wish to be . . . when it comes to visible effort in public—in front of peers . . . student decision-making becomes a high-stakes matter of self-definition in which academic behavior may directly conflict with social identity needs. . . . What matters most is that students come to believe deeply in their own capacity to master difficult academic material through sustained, thoughtful effort. . . . The behaviors cease to be identity watersheds at all because they *no longer set some students off from others*. . . . Every student is completing homework, etc. (p. 589)

Thus, teachers whose classrooms constitute a safe and challenging environment for student learning have artfully combined challenge with support. They know their students well enough to know when a student has blown off an assignment, or when, in contrast, the student simply does not understand a concept well enough to complete high-quality work. When it comes to student commitment to learning, teachers don't take no for an answer, yet they are ready to provide the necessary assistance when that's what's needed. This teaching is not formulaic; it is a high-level professional enterprise in which teachers know when to cajole, when to reteach, when to praise, and when to enlist the participation of

> Teachers whose classrooms constitute a safe and challenging environment for student learning have artfully combined challenge with support.

other students—all in the service of high-level learning within an environment of challenge and support. Within this environment, students persevere in their quest for deep understanding and mastery.

A specific tool used by many teachers for ensuring high-quality work, and for enlisting students in the effort to engage everyone in the work at hand, is to teach students the skills of group work. After all, much important academic work is best done in small groups—discussion, solving problems, completing projects—and such group work, in order to be productive, requires important skills, for example, listening to and respectfully disagreeing with others, assuming tasks for completing work, summarizing the status of a project. Furthermore, students must be able to engage in such work even when not under the direct supervision of the teacher. This is a specific skill and is reflective of a more general classroom culture of productivity. Students are not born with such skills; they need to be explicitly taught and practiced. When they are, they make a material contribution to the culture of productive engagement with high-level work.

When observing in a classroom, then, and initiating a professional conversation, the questions one would seek to explore related to a safe, respectful, and challenging environment could include the following:

- How have you cultivated an environment of respect among the students in this class? What evidence do you have of the effectiveness of the approach?

- How have you worked to cultivate a commitment among the students in this class toward hard work, even in the face of challenges?

- How do you convey to students that while the work in this class is challenging, they'll be able to succeed if they apply themselves?

- What techniques do you use to encourage a culture among students in which they welcome challenging work, rather than seeking an "easy path?"

- Questions about specific observed events related to the classroom environment

Cluster 3: Classroom Management

A fundamental requirement for any productive classroom is that it run smoothly. Teachers must establish efficient procedures for the completion of routine tasks, such as taking attendance, guiding transitions into work groups, distributing and collecting materials, and handling end-of-class dismissal. These procedures accomplish several essential purposes, are taken care of with a minimal loss of instructional time, and provide, for students, the security of familiar routines. Efficient routines convey to students that the teacher is in charge, though not a dictator, thus assuring them that they need not fear chaos.

Classrooms are, after all, crowded places; there are typically over twenty-five students, plus a teacher, in a relatively small space. This fact is a source of anxiety for many new teachers; they fear they will be overwhelmed by the large numbers of students under their care, particularly if the students are physically larger than the teacher. What is to prevent, after all, an outright mutiny, with students simply refusing to comply with the teacher's directions? How to avoid chaos, with students doing whatever they choose, perhaps causing harm to themselves or other students? How can a teacher ensure that students actually *learn* anything? What is to guarantee that students will actually follow the rules, rather than just take charge themselves? These are not unreasonable questions, and a new teacher's anxieties are understandable. In creating and then promulgating classroom routines and procedures, including behavioral norms, a teacher should keep in mind the principles that follow.

Routines and norms should be created with student participation.

Students, like other people, need to feel in control of their lives; they are quickly alienated by a teacher whose approach to classroom management is one of "This is how it is, because I say so." Moreover, classroom routines are established not only to maintain an orderly environment, but to solve real or potential practical problems. Thus, students will readily recognize that since they like to have a chance to speak in a discussion, the challenge is to work out an approach allowing everyone the opportunity to be heard. The same thinking applies to virtually all routines: The question, "What would happen if we all just went for the door at the same time?" will elicit, even from young children, the recognition that the result would be chaotic—chairs could be overturned or some students knocked over. Next can come the question, "What might be some reasonable procedures for leaving the room?"

The attitude of the teacher in establishing routines and procedures is all-important. It's essential that the teacher convey to the students a concern to establish, with them, an environment in which important and interesting work can be accomplished. Therefore, routines and norms are needed for many activities: distributing and collecting materials, keeping a neat classroom, moving between large- and small-group activities, and so on. That is, the purpose of the routines is to maximize student learning; it's not because the teacher insists on control. This attitude permits the teacher to sincerely elicit student contributions.

Routines must be taught.

But even after students and the teacher have developed the routines and norms for how the class will operate, those routines must be taught and practiced. That is, teachers cannot simply assume that their students will automatically know what is intended by a direction such as "Move into your small work groups." Unless students have practiced a routine by which to

> It's essential that the teacher convey to the students a concern to establish, with them, an environment in which important and interesting work can be accomplished.

accomplish such a task, the alternative, given the crowded nature of many classrooms, can be chaos. Thus, experienced teachers devote some time at the beginning of a year to actually *teach* the routines for all sorts of everyday classroom procedures: distributing and collecting materials, pushing chairs in at the end of class, and so on. Teaching routines is the same as teaching other skills: the routine is described, and students have a structured opportunity to practice it (for example, a transition to small groups) and do it again, incorporating feedback about the success of the first attempt. The same also applies to norms of behavior; they can be isolated, and role-played, so that students know what to expect when involved in a situation calling for a teacher to take corrective action. In this way, students are not caught off guard or unprepared by events.

Naturally, without having been in a classroom during the first few days of school, when the classroom routines and procedures were established, an observer can infer only from teacher directions and student actions, whether routines have, in fact, been established earlier in the year. Moreover, those teachers who are fortunate enough to have the assistance of volunteers or paraprofessionals in their classrooms have in addition the challenge of ensuring that those individuals are productively engaged in making a substantive contribution to the life of the class.

When observing in a classroom, then, and initiating a professional conversation, the questions one would seek to explore related to classroom management could include the following:

- To what extent were students involved in establishing the routines and procedures in this class? How did you enlist their participation?

- At the beginning of the school year, which of the procedures did you find it important to actually teach to students? How did you accomplish this?

- To what degree have you succeeded in engaging students themselves in maintaining the routines and procedures? What challenges have you had to overcome in doing this?

- What obstacles have you encountered in engaging students in establishing norms for conduct, and in helping to enforce those norms? What approaches have you found to be most effective?

- Questions about specific observed events related to classroom management

Cluster 4: Student Intellectual Engagement

Student engagement is at the very heart of good teaching; it is typically the first item educators identify when invited to describe the classroom of a teacher whom they consider an expert.

However, the term *engagement* does not have a single, or a simple, definition. First, intellectual engagement is not the same as being busy or on task; it's quite possible for students to be occupied doing work—for example, completing a worksheet—that does not represent new learning. Furthermore, physical activity is not sufficient; an activity might involve students in working with physical materials but doing so in a formulaic manner. The key to student engagement is not physical, but mental, activity. A task might be hands-on. But in order to qualify as intellectual engagement, it must be minds-on. School, in other words, from the point of view of students, is not a spectator sport. Therefore, it's essential to maximize the extent to which students are involved in intellectual activity, such as exploring new ideas, making connections, or formulating and testing hypotheses.

A useful rule of thumb that indicates the degree of student intellectual engagement is the answer to the question "Who's doing the work?" When students listen while the teacher makes a presentation, demonstrates a procedure, or applies a rule, their role may be entirely passive; they may be simply watching while the teacher performs. Not necessarily, however: A teacher may present new material in such a way that students are invited to connect new information with prior understanding or predict outcomes of a scenario. When teachers structure lessons in such a way that students are intellectually active, those students must explore the nuances of meaning of various concepts and generate new understanding. This process involves thinking. Thus, a variation on the maxim "Who's doing the work?" is "Who's doing the thinking?" Only if students are actively thinking (as part of a presentation of content, engaging in a discussion led by the teacher or with classmates or completing a task) can they be said to be intellectually engaged.

In addition to students being engaged in thinking; they can also become aware of their own cognitive processes: that is, teachers can engage students not only in cognitive work, but in *metacognitive* work. How did they arrive at a certain conclusion? What's the evidence for it? In making an error in solving a problem, what was the trajectory of their thinking? Where did it go off track? Can they retrace their steps and find the error? These latter questions deal with the process of thinking and are highly transferable to other situations, and indeed to other subjects. They enable students, when they encounter difficulty through, for example, arriving at a false conclusion, to retrace their steps and take corrective action.

It should also be noted that student engagement in learning does not always appear tidy; when students are wrestling with a new concept or making connections between new content and previously learned material, they may make a few false starts or pursue what turns out to be a dead end before making a course correction. It's challenging for some teachers to allow their students to engage in this *productive struggle,* but the resulting understanding is satisfying to students, empowering them as learners and solidifying their comprehension.

A lesson in which students are engaged usually has a discernible structure: a beginning, a middle, and an end, with scaffolding provided by the teacher or by the activities themselves. The teacher organizes student tasks to provide cognitive challenge and encourages students to reflect on what they have done and what they have learned. That is, the lesson has closure, in which the teacher encourages students to derive important learning from the learning tasks, from the discussion, or from what they have read.

For teachers, there are two critical aspects to teaching for student intellectual engagement: designing (or locating) and managing rich learning tasks and skillfully using student discourse.

Rich learning tasks

Designing (or identifying) suitably demanding learning tasks for students is one of the most challenging aspects of teaching since a task that is challenging for one student may be routine for another. One can analyze the cognitive demand of a task; whether the task is suitably rigorous, or appropriate, for an individual student is determined by the level of knowledge and cognitive development of the student. Thus, a task, in and of itself, is not rigorous or routine; what makes it rigorous or routine is the gap between the demands of the task and the current capabilities of the students who are asked to complete it. If the gap is small or nonexistent, the task is routine and boring; if the gap is too great, the task may be overwhelming. Like Goldilocks's porridge, the gap should be "just right." One technique to address this challenge is to assign tasks with a low bar and a high ceiling—that is, tasks that are accessible to all students, but that, through their expansion, or through the teacher's asking a more demanding follow-up question, can challenge the more-advanced students in the class. Employing this technique is not a simple matter and is developed only after considerable experience.

Another characteristic of rich learning tasks relates to their being "group-worthy," that is, they invite multiple perspectives, which may be represented by the different students working together in group. Much classroom activity, after all, takes place in small groups, with the teacher playing a mediating, rather than a direct teaching role. Tasks that are suitable for group work enable students with different strengths to make a contribution to the overall effort. In order for such work to be productive, of course, students must have acquired the skills of collaboration described in Cluster 2.

> For teachers, there are two critical aspects to teaching for student intellectual engagement: designing (or locating) and managing rich learning tasks and skillfully using student discourse.

Student discourse

Questioning and discussion is used to deepen student understanding (rather than serve as recitation, or a verbal "quiz").

Effective teachers use divergent as well as convergent questions, framed in such a way that they invite students to formulate hypotheses, make connections, or challenge previously held views. These teachers are especially adept at responding to and building on student responses and making use of their ideas.

Class discussions are animated, engaging students in important issues and promoting the use of precise language to deepen and extend understanding. These discussions may be based around questions formulated by the students themselves. Furthermore, when a teacher is building on student responses to questions (whether posed by the teacher or by other students), students are challenged to explain their thinking, to critique the reasoning of others, and to cite specific evidence to back up a position. This focus on argumentation forms the foundation of logical reasoning, a critical skill in all disciplines.

When observing in a classroom, then, and initiating a professional conversation, the questions one would seek to explore related to student engagement could include the following:

- To what extent have you modified the tasks and activities in your adopted curriculum materials to make them more engaging to your students? How have you done that?

- How much of a challenge has it been to teach your students to ask higher-order questions?

- How have you taught your students to engage in discourse with one another? To listen, and disagree with respect?

- To what degree have you succeeded in teaching your students to be aware of their own thinking? How have you done this?

- Are there times when you find you're not able to teach the content you want through engaging activities and learning tasks, when you just have to "lecture through it?" How do you decide when that is needed?

- Questions about specific observed events related to student engagement

Cluster 5: Successful Learning by All Students

It is not sufficient for teachers to engage in an activity called teaching; they must ensure that students learn. That is, one way of defining *teaching* is as "that which causes student learning." While this appears an obvious statement, it is frequently overlooked by educators as they attempt to codify *good teaching* in ways that focus exclusively on the actions of teachers without considering the success of those efforts in ensuring student learning.

Teachers recognize that all learning is complex, involving the interplay of conceptual and procedural knowledge, facts and processes, dispositions and habits of mind. Students don't master all of these in the same way, or in the same sequence, and they enter any lesson with their own strengths and areas for growth. However, every lesson and longer unit has a focus, and it's in that area of focus that teachers must be able to articulate, and make specific plans to address, what they intend students to learn.

Ascertaining whether students have, in fact, learned what was intended requires the design (or adoption) of summative assessments aligned to those outcomes (so that the teacher can take corrective action before moving on), and formative assessments to be used, on short notice, during the course of a lesson. This requires sophisticated record-keeping systems. In addition, in order for teachers to modify their approach to ensure that all students are making progress toward the instructional purposes of the lesson, they must not only be aware of resources (in the school or, more broadly, in the district or the community) that can be brought to bear. They also must be committed to do what is needed to help every student succeed.

Traditionally, teachers did not ascertain the extent to which their students had learned the material being taught until they had completed an instructional unit; indeed, the assessment (usually a test of some type) signaled the end of instruction, students' work was graded, and the class went on to the next unit. In this approach, teachers could know whether or to what extent their students *had* learned but could not ensure that they did so. Fortunately, many teachers now employ a subtler approach, one designed to shape instruction during the course of a lesson. Teachers monitor students' responses and activities constantly, monitoring the pulse of the class frequently during a lesson and making revisions to their approach when needed. These changes might take the form of making a slight modification in the place of an activity or in the activity itself, based on students' indications of lack of comprehension (too challenging) or boredom (too easy). Such monitoring occurs constantly and is not specifically planned.

However, other techniques used by teachers may be, indeed must be, planned in advance. This is useful to monitor, for example, students' understanding of a particularly difficult concept. In that case students' responses to a carefully crafted question, with their answers written on whiteboards and held up for the teacher to see, provide important diagnostic information—about individual students—to the teacher about the extent of their understanding. Such assessment becomes completely integrated into instruction, with teachers alert to what's going on during a lesson, watching students for indications that they are following the discussion or that they are acquiring the desired understanding from an instructional activity. Sometimes students provide such indications explicitly; they ask clarifying questions, for example. On other occasions, however, the indications are much more subtle or camouflaged, for example, a quizzical look.

Another important mechanism to ensure students' success is arranging for them to receive specific and timely feedback on their efforts. This feedback can be provided, of course, by the teacher. But it can also be supplied by other students (as when they challenge—respectfully—the thinking of their classmates), or by the instructional activities themselves. For example, the solution to a problem in mathematics may simply not work. Whatever the source of the feedback, students come to realize that learning is a process of continual iteration; it's never complete.

Families, too, can be allies in a teacher's quest to ensure student success. They have, after all, known the students for a longer time than has the teacher and can provide insight into the students' lives and interests beyond school. Such information can be invaluable to a teacher in planning instruction and responding to individuals.

Attention to every student's learning is grounded in some important assumptions, namely, that the students are capable of high-level learning and that the teacher has the necessary skill, resources, and attitude to enable them to succeed. These beliefs are fundamental; if teachers lack a strong sense of efficacy, they will be inclined to give up easily when students experience difficulty (as virtually all students do). In such cases, teachers find other factors on which to place the "blame" for students' struggles: their backgrounds ("His parents are getting a divorce.") the perceived weaknesses of older siblings ("Her brother never could do fractions either."), the lack of skill of a previous teacher ("They should have learned this last year."), or the inadequacy of the adopted materials ("This textbook is terrible.").Therefore, teachers' ensuring the learning of every student is a reflection of their confidence that they can teach well and that their students are capable of high-level learning.

When observing in a classroom, then, and initiating a professional conversation, the questions one would seek to explore related to successful learning by all students could include the following:

- How are you sure that all the important learning outcomes in your curriculum are included in summative assessments?

- What techniques do you use, in addition to those I observed, to make sure that all your students are "with" you during a lesson?

- Describe a strategy you developed, before a lesson, to use at a critical point in that lesson, to check on the level of understanding of all your students.

- What steps do you take to challenge your more advanced students?

> Attention to every student's learning is grounded in some important assumptions, namely, that the students are capable of high-level learning and that the teacher has the necessary skill, resources, and attitude to enable them to succeed.

- To what extent have you found that it's important to engage parents in ensuring successful learning by all your students?

- Questions about specific observed events related to successful learning by all students

Cluster 6: Professionalism

Schools are, first of all, environments to promote the learning of students. But they are also places for the intellectual engagement of teachers so that they can better promote the learning of their students. Schools are, in other words, learning organizations for teachers, whose full potential is realized only when they regard themselves as members of a professional community. This community is characterized by mutual support and respect, as well as by recognition of the responsibility of all teachers to be constantly seeking ways to improve their practice and to contribute to the life of the school and to the broader professional community. Inevitably, teachers' duties extend beyond the doors of their classrooms and include activities related to the entire school or larger district, or both. These activities include such things as service on school and district curriculum committees or engagement with the parent-teacher organization. With experience, teachers assume leadership roles in these activities.

As in other professions, the complexity of teaching requires continued growth and development in order for teachers to keep their knowledge and skills current. Continuing to stay informed and increasing their skills allows teachers to become even more effective and to exercise leadership among their colleagues. constantly refine their understanding of how to engage students in learning; thus, growth in content, and content-specific pedagogy are essential to good teaching. And to the extent that information technology is an aid to student mathematics learning, it's essential for teachers to stay abreast of developments in that area as well.

Networking with colleagues through such activities as joint planning, study groups, and lesson study provides opportunities for teachers to learn from one another. In particular, joint examination of student work provides invaluable insight into the cognitive processes of individual students as they wrestle with concepts that are not available in any other way. These activities allow for job-embedded professional development. In addition, professional educators increase their effectiveness in the classroom by belonging to professional organizations (at the regional, state, or even national level), reading professional journals, attending educational conferences, and taking university classes. As they gain experience and expertise, educators find ways to contribute to their colleagues and to the profession.

> Schools are learning organizations for teachers, whose full potential is realized only when they regard themselves as members of a professional community.

Expert teachers also demonstrate professionalism in service both to students and to the profession. Teaching at the highest levels of performance requires that teachers remain focused on students, putting them first regardless of how this stance might challenge long-held assumptions, past practice, or simply an easier or more convenient procedure. For example, dialogue around the issues surrounding the appropriate use of homework is certain to be spirited, and reveal teachers' deep belief about student learning and how best to support it.

Accomplished teachers have a strong moral compass and are guided by what is in the best interest of each student, even when this ethos involves challenging long-established school policies or procedures. They display professionalism in a number of ways. For example, they conduct interactions with colleagues in a manner notable for honesty and integrity. Furthermore, they know their students' needs and can readily access resources with which to step in and provide help that may extend beyond the classroom. Seeking greater flexibility in the ways school rules and policies are applied, expert teachers advocate for their students in ways that might challenge traditional views and the educational establishment. They also display professionalism in the ways they approach problem solving and decision making, with student needs constantly in mind. Finally, accomplished teachers consistently adhere to school and district policies and procedures but are willing to work to improve those that may be outdated or ineffective.

When in a professional conversation about professionalism, the questions one would seek to explore could include the following:

- How do you stay abreast of the subjects you teach?

- In what ways have you contributed to the professional environment of your grade or department or the entire school?

- Can you describe an occasion when you, out of concern for the welfare of your students, challenged the thinking of your colleagues?

- What resources, within the school or district, or even in the larger community, have you enlisted to help one (or more) of yours students?

- How have you taken a leadership role within your grade or department to support the learning of your colleagues?

Summary

The topics for conversation are derived from the big ideas from Chapter 3 and, indeed, serve as the practical manifestations of those ideas. As part of the intellectual culture of every school, it's important that teachers know that these ideas, and their derivative topics, are always relevant to a conversation. They play out, of course, differently, in different settings (that's one of the reasons the conversations are interesting). But they are always in play and form the basis for rich professional dialogue.

As part of the exploration of the topics for conversation, it's important for teachers to identify how these ideas are manifested in their own practice. In order for professional conversations to be productive, it's important that teachers do not feel they are being judged in their teaching whenever an administrator visits. Rather, these topics are always available to explore what is happening in a lesson and how it might be strengthened. They represent the challenges of teaching, which, given the complexity of the work, can always be improved.

5 Conversation Skills

Conversations about practice constitute a critical vehicle for professional learning by teachers; conducting those conversations, then, is an essential activity for those in leadership positions in the school: site administrators, department chairs, team leaders, and instructional coaches. But it's not sufficient, or even appropriate, to arrive at a teacher's door after school and simply blurt out an impression of what one has observed during a lesson. Professional conversations require skills, and learning those skills is an important obligation of school leaders.

Setting the Tone for Conversation

Naturally, conversations about practice occur within the context of the school's culture; therefore, establishing and maintaining a healthy and productive professional culture is essential to the success and richness of professional conversations. This culture consists of a number of interlocking factors in which setting the proper tone is critical.

The importance of establishing trust among teachers and between teachers and administrators has been described in Chapter 2, "Power and Leadership in Schools." Furthermore, the importance of creating and maintaining a learning organization has been addressed. One of the principal characteristics of a learning organization is that everyone accepts the obligation to engage in ongoing professional learning, that teaching is such challenging and complex work that it is impossible to do perfectly. This suggests that teaching, no matter how successful, could always be improved; professional conversations are an important vehicle for such professional learning.

Interestingly, many of the insights regarding professional conversation are derived from the literature in the business world. It would seem that even in a for-profit company, enlightened practice by supervisors is highly consistent with that of administrators in nonprofit agencies (including schools), derived from a culture of shared goals and professional respect.

Even in the business environment, where organizations are typically organized in a stricter hierarchical fashion than are schools, analysts recognize the importance of setting the tone for productive conversation. In some ways, it's not necessary; supervisors are, after all, the boss: They have a right to it. On the other hand, by approaching a subordinate with humility and asking permission to discuss a professional situation, the manager conveys respect for that subordinate. David Rock (2006), a leader in the field of business communication, points out the importance of establishing the right tone: "When you are in a position of power and establish permission anyway, it can have a big positive impact on work relationships. It builds trust, and because people feel safer around you they are likely to open up more" (p. 115).

What is true in the business environment is doubly the case in professional organizations such as schools. The fact that the principal is the boss does not guarantee that teachers will be inclined to engage in in-depth conversations about practice; the principal can approach a teacher for such a conversation, but if the culture is not conducive for risk taking, the teacher will be inclined to play it safe and take as few chances as possible. That is, although the principal or supervisor's position of formal authority can guarantee that teachers must engage in conversations, that position cannot ensure that the conversations are productive; only a safe environment and skill on the part of the principal can accomplish that.

> A principal or supervisor's position of authority cannot guarantee productive conversations; only a safe environment and skill on the part of the principal can accomplish that.

By demonstrating respect for the teacher's perspective and by maintaining the focus on the big ideas described in Chapter 3, a principal or supervisor can assume a problem-solving rather than an authoritarian approach. The outcome of a productive professional conversation is exploration of how a lesson could have been strengthened, based on the big ideas. It is not a matter of a principal insisting on a particular approach to teaching; instead, the principal and teacher consider together, based on what has transpired during a lesson, how to improve student engagement and learning in subsequent instructional encounters. The principal and teacher, in other words, are on the same side, examining a situation together, considering "problems of practice." Far from being adversaries, the two are educators together, sharing perspectives and working to address the myriad challenges that every lesson presents.

Linguistic Skills

The outcome of a professional conversation depends, overwhelmingly, on the skill of the individual leading the conversation. Whether that person is an administrator, supervisor, mentor, or coach, the goal of the conversation is to enable a teacher to think through a given issue in an open, professional manner. This goal is made more challenging when a school is organized in a rigid, hierarchical manner, with power perceived as emanating from the principal's office; it's more likely to occur within an environment and culture of trust and mutual respect. The most important linguistic skill for administrators and supervisors lies in asking the right questions and asking them in the right manner. Depending on the culture in the school, any question asked by an administrator has the potential to sound, to teachers, like an order—or, almost as damaging—as making a suggestion that a teacher feels must be followed.

Researchers in the business community also recognize the critical nature of linguistic skills by supervisors. As David Rock (2006) writes, "Learning to ask powerful questions is the most central skill in this book. When we ask the right questions, people . . . reflect and their brains go into the alpha state. If we ask enough of the right questions, people have their own aha" (p. 124). The alpha state is related to reflection. "You can clearly tell when someone is reflecting on an issue: his or her face changes. Most people look up or slightly up and across and get a dazed look on their face. . . . nearly everyone becomes very silent for a moment" (p. 106). Tom Peters and Nancy Austin (1985) also caution against the perception by subordinates that any question from the boss sounds like a command; it requires enormous skill to ask a question in such a way that it does not suggest providing direction.

There are a number of intertwined elements of skillful questioning and conversation that promote teacher thinking. To some extent, they may be considered in isolation from one another, although they are frequently combined in practice. The blend of tools affects the teacher's emotions and cognition (Lipton & Wellman, 2000). They are described below.

Establishing Rapport

Body language and tone of voice can be as important as the words actually spoken in establishing trust and rapport between people. A posture of leaning in conveys interest in what the other person is saying. Many teachers have discovered the power of tone of voice when speaking to students; there is a big difference between "Did you get a B on that test?" or "Did *you* get a B on that test?" or "Did you get a *B* on that test?" The first question is neutral, the second expresses surprise that the student did so well (or perhaps so poorly), while the third expresses skepticism about the validity of the student's grade. The same principle applies to conversations among adults: A sarcastic or skeptical tone of voice undermines rapport and professional respect, as in "What's going on in here?" spoken in an accusatory tone. Inflection on particular words can result in defensiveness on the part of the teacher.

Much of the rapport between teachers and administrators is established in the general culture of the school in honoring

> The most important linguistic skill for administrators and supervisors lies in asking the right questions and asking them in the right manner.

professionalism and self-directed inquiry (described earlier). But this rapport is also reinforced, or undermined, every day, as part of every conversation; it is conveyed through expressions of interest in the teacher's perspective, the teacher's expertise, and the teacher's good intentions. Just as teachers establish rapport in their classrooms with students by conveying the sense that every student is important and valued, administrators establish that rapport with teachers (and other adults, as well as children) in their schools.

Using Positive Presuppositions

The manner in which a question is asked implies much about a questioner's assumptions. The classic "When did you stop beating your wife?" suggests that it is being addressed to a wife batterer. The question "In what ways do you learn about your students' interests outside of school?" assumes that the teacher has made the effort to acquire such information. Alternatively, "What are some patterns you see from these student work samples?" suggests that the supervisor or coach expects that the teacher will have been alert to such patterns and will, in fact, have noticed them. Even if the inquiry is open ended, the supervisor needs to be cautious about not questioning the capabilities of the teacher "by communicating doubt in the teacher's awareness and ability to address the topic" (Lipton & Wellman, 2000, p. 32).

Teachers can easily detect negative presuppositions. For example, "Do these students always behave so badly?" indicates that the students are behaving badly and may suggest that the supervisor or coach believes that the teacher has not taken adequate steps to teach them better patterns of behavior. Ironically, of course, such a question may have been well intentioned; the supervisor may have meant to convey sympathy for the teacher's predicament in working with a difficult class. But word choice is important, and unless the supervisor specifically expresses that sympathy (as in, for example, "My, what a challenge you have with this combination of students!"), many teachers will interpret an offhand comment as veiled criticism.

Inviting and Sustaining Thinking

An important purpose of all professional conversations is to extend teachers' thinking about their practice; this can only happen if the conversations occur in a safe environment. At the same time, supervisors and coaches can help teachers stretch their thinking into new areas. Several specific techniques can help in this endeavor.

Nondichotomous questions. By avoiding questions with a simple yes or no (i.e., single-word) answer, supervisors and coaches signal that they are interested in deeper conversations. Dichotomous questions tend to shut down thinking; once the answer is given, that tends to be the end of the matter. However, even a simplistic answer can be shaped in such a way that the teacher must become more thoughtful. For example, if a teacher responds to a question with a simple yes or no or one-word answer, the supervisor or coach can invite further thinking with just a tilt of the head or a comment such as "Tell me more about that."

> An important purpose of all professional conversations is to extend teachers' thinking about their practice.

Plural forms. By asking questions in the form "What are some possible explanations for . . . ?" or "What factors do you consider when planning . . . ?" a supervisor or coach signals that there is not a single correct answer to the question and that the teacher can engage in deeper thinking about it. Using plural forms conveys that there are many possible responses and that they are all worthy of consideration.

Promoting analytic thinking. Supervisors and coaches can extend teachers' thinking by asking questions that invite teachers to dig into their observations, with the aim of learning more from them. Thus, a follow-up question to a teacher's statement about, for example, the students' failures to complete homework assignments on time might ask, "What patterns have you noticed? Which days of the week seem to be most difficult?" or "What might be some possible explanations . . . ?" Such questions require that teachers compare one situation with another, identify patterns, or interpret events. And by using invitational language and tone, the supervisor or coach suggests that there is not a single correct answer to the question.

Arthur Costa and Robert Garmston (2002) point out that the form of questions can make a significant difference in the sort of thinking that results from the questions asked by supervisors and coaches. They argue that questions structured as "'would/if' kinds of questions cause the brain to create, dream, visualize, evaluate, speculate, and imagine. Those two little words carry great power. They cause the brain to think hypothetically, to change circumstances, and to predict alternative outcomes" (p. 111).

Encouraging metacognition. Metacognition refers to a person's thinking, not about the events under consideration but about one's own thinking about those events. By helping teachers *go meta*, supervisors and coaches enable them to extract general principles from their experience and to see how their own thinking about it has evolved. Hence, a question such as "In what ways could you describe your students' understanding of place value?" can transition into a metacognitive question such as "How has your assessment of your students' understanding of place value evolved during the past year?"

Examining assumptions and implications. All decisions made by teachers are grounded in certain assumptions about learning and teaching. However, most teachers are not accustomed to examining these assumptions or to exploring their implications for future practice. Chapter 3, "The Big Ideas That Shape Professional Conversations," describes recent research in learning and motivation; a useful series of questions can help teachers examine the implications of these findings for daily classroom life. For example, a supervisor or coach might make the observation that "Reflecting on your use of student choice in designing learning activities, in what ways have you found it to be effective? " or "Recalling that mastery of complex content is satisfying to students, how might you devise activities that tap into that natural drive?" Such questions don't assume any single correct answer. Indeed, they don't suggest that there even *is* an answer, but they hold the promise of opening up an important line of conversation.

Probing

When supervisors or coaches probe a teacher's thinking, they encourage teachers to dig deeper, to explain their thinking. Probes include such statements as "Could you talk more about that?" or "Could you give me an example of what you mean?" or simply, "Tell me more about that . . . ."

A powerful approach to probing is silence, simply saying nothing. Just as in the classroom, using wait time is an effective strategy to encourage deeper student thinking, so silence can enable teachers to extend their thinking. And just as waiting (even five seconds) for a student to respond can feel like an eternity, so can silence in a professional conversation feel very long. But it is powerful and can be employed at several stages in a conversation. By waiting following a teacher's statement, supervisors or coaches indicate that they believe that the teacher has more to say on the subject. And indeed, they frequently do. By pausing prior to responding, supervisors or coaches indicate that they must think prior to saying anything; this practice models thoughtfulness and reflection.

Paraphrasing

One of the most important linguistic skills for supervisors and coaches is that of paraphrasing. When one paraphrases a statement, one repeats it in a slightly different manner; this invites teachers to hear an account of what they have just said and to recognize any mismatch between what they thought they said and what was understood. But almost more important, paraphrasing sends three very important messages to a teacher. By paraphrasing what a teacher has said, supervisors or coaches indicate that they have heard what the teacher has said, that they understand what was said, and that they care. In some respects, the last message, the caring, is the most important because it contributes to the sense of rapport and trust between the teacher and supervisor or coach.

Some experts in coaching maintain that every statement by a teacher should be paraphrased before the conversation proceeds. By building in these pauses, supervisors or coaches indicate that they are trying to understand the teacher's point of view; in an important respect, it places the teacher and the supervisor on the same side of an issue or question, which they are trying to understand together. Without the paraphrasing, a series of questions can quickly become an interrogation or at least feel like one to a teacher.

Paraphrasing can take several forms, reflecting somewhat different purposes (Lipton & Wellman, 2000, pp. 40–42).

Acknowledging and clarifying. A supervisor or coach might restate in his or her own words a teacher's comment and say, in response to a teacher's statement, "In other words, . . ." or "I'm not sure I understand what you are saying. Did you mean that . . . ?" Such a paraphrase acknowledges the teacher's situation and honors the teacher's perspective. It conveys a desire to see events from the teacher's point of view, rather than imposing that of the coach or supervisor. Sometimes, clarifying involves putting the question back to the teacher for further elaboration, as in "Could you explain that a bit further?" or "Could you give me an example of what you mean?" Such an exchange would then be followed by a further paraphrase by the supervisor or coach, for example, "So what you mean is . . . ."

Summarizing and organizing. Paraphrasing can also involve summarizing a number of small items with a more general statement, as in "You seem to be saying that your students don't demonstrate respect for one another. Do you think that's an accurate summary of your comments?"

A very useful linguistic technique in paraphrasing, for summarizing and organizing, is to shift the level of abstraction either up or down. When supervisors or coaches shift up, they interpret a number of specific teacher comments into a more general principle, such as "Those events suggest that you're seeing a lot of examples of your students' natural curiosity. What do you think?" Such upward shifts of focus can help those teachers who tend to think in concrete, sequential ways to see the bigger picture, to appreciate that what they are observing are examples of larger principles.

Downward shifts can be very useful as well. In employing the strategy of downward shifts of focus, a supervisor or coach invites a teacher (particularly one who tends to think in global terms) to provide some specific examples or to think about how a certain approach in mathematics, for example, could be applied in social studies.

Summary

Professional conversations, as noted in earlier chapters, are a critical vehicle for promoting professional learning. But educators are not born with the skill to conduct productive conversations, particularly when the dynamics of the unequal power relationship between teachers and administrators are factored into the equation.

Conducting productive conversations requires a positive culture. But it also requires skill, particularly on the part of leaders, whether they're administrators, instructional coaches, or peers. Those skills include setting the tone, inviting thinking, and the employment of linguistic skills that enable teachers to explore their practice.

How these skills are used in the conduct of informal professional conversations is the subject of the next chapter.

6 Informal Professional Conversations

Informal professional conversations are those held between a teacher and another educator following an informal, drop-in observation. Such observations are typically rather brief, perhaps as short as five minutes, and are always unannounced. The observers may be any educator in the school—a colleague, a coach, a supervisor, or an administrator—although most frequently they are supervisors or administrators (or instructional coaches who have no—or very light—instructional duties of their own) for the simple reason that those individuals normally have the flexibility to visit classrooms as part of their daily routine.

Most supervisors and administrators eagerly accept their responsibility to serve as the instructional leader of the school, to offer guidance and support to teachers. However, many of them are baffled as to exactly how to do that, particularly in the context of informal observations. They can walk in and out of classrooms and stay for a portion of the lesson, but then what? How and when do they have a professional conversation with the teacher about what they observed? In particular, how do they conduct those conversations in such a manner that teachers don't feel judged? Should the supervisor or administrator offer feedback? If so, what is its purpose? This chapter offers guidance on these important questions.

Informal classroom observations by school leaders and subsequent professional conversations are not part of the culture of most schools, as described by Megan Tschannen-Moran (2004):

> On the first day of school I visited every classroom. I continued to visit each classroom every day the first week of school just for a short visit to get a feel for the building and to be visible. Early the next week I was visited by a teacher who spoke for herself and 'others' and explained to me that it was not the practice of that building principal

to visit classrooms without an appointment. I explained that I could not make good decisions for the school community without being in classrooms and suggested she pass the word. I showed her the list I had made of things that I could do to improve the learning environment, things like repair of clocks, moving old books, etc. That changed her attitude. (p. 109)

The practice by supervisors and administrators to be out and about in the school, to be visible, to be in a position to engage in genuine professional conversations, is at the heart of a culture of professional inquiry. In addition, however, it's critical that a common understanding of good practice provide the underpinning of such conversations; as described in Chapter 3, "The Big Ideas," important shared views of student learning and how to best promote it provide the mental map for both teachers and administrators regarding practice. It is through professional conversations that such ideas are realized.

Purpose

The principle purpose of informal professional conversations is to engage teachers in in-depth reflection regarding the events of a learning experience observed in their classrooms. As its name suggests, both the observation and the conversation are *informal;* that is, they don't follow any established protocol and are not conducted as part of the school or district's formal process of teacher evaluation. Instead, their purpose is purely *professional;* there is no administrative or compliance purpose served by the observations and conversations. That is, the informal observation and the ensuing conversation are nonevaluative. By conducting informal observations, supervisors and administrators keep their finger on the pulse regarding instruction in each teacher's classroom; what they observe provides rich raw material for professional conversation. In general, therefore, supervisors and administrators have removed their evaluator hat when they conduct informal observations, particularly for tenured teachers.

Naturally, it's possible that a teacher's practice, as observed in an informal observation, might show serious deficiencies that require corrective action by the administrator. In that case, the administrator must put the evaluator hat back on and proceed as outlined in the district's system of performance appraisal. Such a scenario, however unlikely, is possible. Thus, whenever a supervisor or administrator darkens the door, many teachers are likely to experience a tightening of the stomach muscles and will probably take a quick glance around the room to determine how it is likely to look to the visitor. This reality reflects

> The principle purpose of informal professional conversations is to engage teachers in in-depth reflection regarding the events of a learning experience observed in their classrooms.

the inherent tension between power and leadership; a principal, intending to exercise professional leadership, becomes caught in a teacher's fear of the principal's irresponsible use of power.

Informal professional conversations, then, if they are to be rich, must occur in a culture in which everyone recognizes the nature of power in a professional organization and the responsibility of those with positional authority to use that authority to promote high levels of student engagement and learning. That can only occur if conversations about practice are conducted in an environment of trust and respect, and the conversations challenge the thinking of both parties to the conversation. They are professional dialogues, in which each individual has important perspectives to bring, within the framework of shared understandings of the big ideas.

Settings for Professional Conversations

The individuals involved with teachers in informal professional conversations are principally those who have sufficient flexibility in their schedules to permit them to visit classrooms—typically administrators, supervisors, or instructional coaches. As will be evident from the following section, the nature of the conversation depends quite heavily on whether the teacher is tenured or nontenured and whether the observer is someone in a supervisory capacity. And the employment status of a teacher has an important consequence on the nature of informal professional conversations; tenured teachers are more secure in their situation and are, thus, less threatened by the presence of a visitor in their classrooms than are nontenured teachers.

There are four distinct settings in which informal professional conversations may occur: those between non-tenured teachers and a nonsupervisory colleague, those between a nontenured teacher and a supervisor, those between a tenured teacher and a nonsupervisory colleague, and those between a tenured teacher and a supervisor. These will each be described briefly below.

Nontenured Teacher and a
Nonsupervisory Colleague, Such as an Instructional Coach

As has been noted previously, nontenured teachers are, of necessity, vulnerable in their positions and are therefore likely to be highly sensitive to the perceived perceptions of anyone in authority, such as a principal or supervisor. On the other hand, with nonsupervisory colleagues, they can be natural and can feel free to admit their own weaknesses or seek the other's thoughts on aspects of their teaching in which they are not yet confidant.

When nonsupervisory colleagues informally visit the classes of nontenured teachers, their observations are governed by the big ideas described in Chapter 3. But because the teachers hold a probationary contract, the observers will be alert to the teachers' need to receive support, reassurance, and, perhaps, some useful coaching on their general teaching skills. The teachers will appreciate tips that their more experienced colleague can offer and will welcome the opportunity to explore issues of concern to them, but always in the context of the big ideas. That is, what implications does the research on student learning and motivation, classroom culture, and the nature of student engagement have for the design of learning experiences? In this setting, the conversation is one of joint problem solving: How can we bring what we know about the big ideas to bear on the work of students and teachers?

Nontenured Teacher and a Supervisor

Informal professional conversations between nontenured teachers and supervisors are fundamentally different from those with nonsupervisory colleagues. Nontenured teachers are, after all, insecure in their employment; even if an administrator has provided informal assurances of success, while their status is that of probation, nontenured teachers feel vulnerable. Teaching contracts for nontenured teachers, as reflected in most negotiated agreements, may be not be renewed, after all, for any or even no reason. Thus, any interaction between nontenured teachers and a supervisor can be dangerous territory for the teacher; until trust is established, the teacher is likely to feel at risk.

Thus, the nature of the conversation between a supervisor and a nontenured teacher is one of, as Megan Tschannen-Moran (2004) has described it, an "artful combination of support and challenge" (p. 109). That is, the supervisor's role is one of, first of all, offering reassurance to the new teacher; teaching is, after all, immensely complex, and new teachers frequently feel insecure in their skill. On the other hand, the conversations are important to both probe the teacher's thinking and promote structured reflection.

Some supervisors will sense that they should not push nontenured teachers as hard as they would tenured teachers; they may feel that the probationary teachers can't, in some sense, take it. But it's a pity to miss the opportunity for professional learning afforded by these informal conversations. It's not easy, to be sure, to offer an optimal combination of support and challenge. It depends, as does so much else, on the professional culture established in the school. And it depends, as will be described in a later section of this chapter, on the manner in which the lesson is discussed. It's not a matter of the supervisor offering a critique of what

> The conversation is one of joint problem solving: How can we bring what we know about the big ideas to bear on the work of students and teachers?

was observed or of offering soft-pedaled feedback; rather, the two individuals discuss, together, the observed events in light of the big ideas from Chapter 3.

Although more difficult to achieve than between nontenured teachers and nonsupervisory colleagues, the goal of the conversation between nontenured teachers and administrators is the same. The supervisor and the teacher are two educators, both trying to enhance the opportunities for learning by students in the class. Thus, what was the purpose of the lesson? Within the context of the teacher's instructional purpose, what was the nature of what the students were doing? What was its level of intellectual rigor? To what extent were the students engaged in meaningful work? If any of these aspects of the instruction could have been better, then what are some possible ways in which they could have been strengthened? The supervisor is not judging the teacher but engaging in joint problem solving, with the teacher proposing many of the ideas.

> The supervisor and the teacher are two educators, both trying to enhance the opportunities for learning by students in the class.

Tenured Teacher and a Nonsupervisory Colleague, Such as an Instructional Coach

The setting of the tenured teacher and a nonsupervisory colleague is the most conducive to informal professional conversation because the teacher's situation is secure and the colleague, in any event, is not in a supervisory relationship to the teacher. The main challenge in this setting is for the teachers to make conversation sufficiently rigorous to be meaningful. It is frequently tempting for teachers, when they engage in informal conversation, to let their conversation wander, to meander through topics. This is particularly the case if teachers work closely together or if they are friends outside of school. It requires a certain discipline to keep one's attention focused on important (and sometimes challenging) professional issues. On the other hand, when this is achieved, the resulting conversations tend to be highly rewarding for both individuals.

The key to a productive conversation lies in the degree to which the big ideas have permeated the culture of the school, providing the lens through which classroom events are viewed. When those big ideas have been established as the school's currency, then conversations between teachers, even when neither holds positional authority over the other, make use of those concepts. The big ideas themselves and their implications for classroom practice provide the architecture for professional conversation.

Tenured Teacher and a Supervisor

Professional conversations between tenured teachers and a supervisor have the potential to be very rich and invigorating. Although the supervisor does have nominal authority over the

The key to a productive conversation lies in the degree to which the big ideas have permeated the culture of the school, providing the lens through which classroom events are viewed.

teacher, the fact that the teacher is tenured provides the teacher with a high degree of stability and security. That is, it is a relatively low-risk environment for the teacher, which means that the conversation can follow fruitful professional paths as they present themselves. However, because the supervisor (principal, supervisor, or department chair) has the responsibility to evaluate the teacher's performance, the interaction typically takes place with greater energy than is the case between teacher colleagues.

When the big ideas have been established and when they permeate the culture of the school, those ideas and the topics for conversation that flow from them provide the natural subject matter for informal conversations. All those ideas are on the table and may be addressed at any time in conversations initiated by those in a supervisory capacity. But the fact that such topics may be addressed at any time does not suggest that teachers should be placed in a defensive posture with respect to them. Rather, the conversations take place within an environment of a quest: "How can these important big ideas play out in our classrooms?" "If it's important for students to be engaged in meaningful work, what is a question I could use to introduce this activity that would draw them into it, that would intrigue them?" These are questions that lend themselves to a problem-solving mentality. The teacher is not performing for the supervisor; rather, they are two educators engaged in a mutual quest for better practice.

Procedure

Informal professional conversations follow brief drop-in observations usually conducted by administrators or supervisors. The observations themselves are unannounced and may reflect a principal's practice of visiting classrooms on a regular basis. Alternatively, the visits might be a bit more structured in nature, with a principal making a commitment to visit, for example, five classrooms every day for a period of fifteen minutes each.

But whatever the nature of the classroom visits, following an observation, supervisors and administrators are faced with a challenge: how to talk about what they have observed there in such a manner that it yields the maximum benefit to teachers. How, in other words, to help teachers stretch their thinking without coming across as critical or judgmental.

The conversations take place within an environment of a quest: "How can these important big ideas play out in our classrooms?"

Informal professional conversations are best conducted in an informal manner, possibly even in the lunchroom or faculty lounge. Some might object to this because the conversation is then, of necessity, public. However, conducting the conversations in a public space reinforces the notion that instruction and the challenges encountered in designing and executing meaningful instructional plans are not a private affair but are part of the shared business of the school. Challenges confronting individual teachers, particularly those related to the big ideas, are similar to those being addressed by all teachers. Everyone sitting around the lunch table will have dealt with similar issues, and if they choose to participate, colleagues can serve as informal resources.

The Observation

Administrators and supervisors, when they make brief, informal observations, aim to be as unobtrusive in the classroom as possible. That is, on entering a classroom, it's important not to attract attention to oneself or to assume a stern demeanor. The observer is there out of interest, to learn how the teacher has organized the classroom for student learning, to get a sense of what the students are doing and how they are engaging with the content. If a teacher (sometimes out of nervousness) attempts to make an introduction to the class, it might be advisable to say something like, "Please carry on with what you're doing; I'm just visiting for a few minutes."

The big ideas are reflected in classroom events in a number of distinct ways, any of which yield interesting raw material for analysis and discussion. In fact, the areas of classroom practice particularly rich for analysis were described in considerable detail in Chapter 4, "The Topics for Conversation," as

- clarity of instructional purpose and accuracy of content,
- safe, respectful, supportive, and challenging learning environment,
- classroom management,
- student intellectual engagement,
- successful learning by all students, and
- professionalism.

The big ideas described in Chapter 3 have enormous impact on everything that happens in classrooms. They affect what teachers decide to focus on in a lesson, how students are engaged in high-level learning, and how the principles of motivation can be applied. Educators know (from their understanding of the big ideas) that students learn through their active intellectual engagement with important content. That is, they learn not through what the *teacher* does but through what *they* do, how they engage with interesting questions and issues, and how they consolidate their learning through structured reflection and extension.

In addition, the most powerful source of student motivation is intrinsic; children are naturally very curious, and it is one of the challenges of schools to help them retain that attitude toward the world and to acquire important knowledge and skill. Last, students who hold a malleable, rather than a fixed, view of intelligence are far more likely to persevere in challenging work and to be successful in their studies.

Thus, when supervisors or administrators enter a classroom to conduct an informal observation, they are not checking off, in their minds, which of the professional teaching standards (such as in the framework for teaching) the teacher is demonstrating. Rather, they turn their attention to the bigger clusters of those standards, and rather than watching the teacher, they pay close attention to the students. It's helpful if supervisors ask themselves the following questions:

- What are the students doing? What is its level of cognitive challenge?

- Is what students are doing inherently interesting?

- What are the students probably learning from doing this? I wonder if that learning is what the teacher intended.

- How are the students encouraged to persevere in their approaches to learning complex material?

- To what extent do the students appear to assume responsibility for their learning and conduct?

- Is the environment a safe one for students to take risks? To what extent do they support one another? How does the teacher show respect for each student's intellect?

- To what extent is the classroom a smooth and well-organized environment?

- If there are school and district initiatives one would expect to observe, are they in evidence?

The Conversation

When discussing the events of a classroom visit with a teacher following a brief observation, the supervisor or administrator uses all the linguistic skills described in Chapter 5. These include establishing rapport, using positive presuppositions, inviting and sustaining thinking (through techniques such as using nondichotomous questions and plural forms, promoting analytic thinking, encouraging metacognition, examining assumptions and implications), probing, and using paraphrasing. These skills are essential to nonthreatening conversation.

But as important is the culture of inquiry established in the school. For professional conversations to be nonthreatening, it's essential that all educators have had the opportunity to establish, together, their common expectations about the nature of learning in the school. This is a critical responsibility of leadership, to have worked with the professional staff to study the big ideas and topics for conversation, as well as the concepts embedded in the school's professional teaching standards, to establish the school's common approach to learning and teaching.

Once that has occurred, they are on the table; they are all fair game for conversation. Thus, when a supervisor asks a question in which a teacher would demonstrate, for example, clarity of focus, it's not because the supervisor has any reason to believe that the teacher is deficient in this regard. Instead, it's because all teachers, at all times, should have such clarity; they should be able to explain what they are trying to achieve (i.e., what student learning they are attempting to promote) and how they are going about it. An essential aspect of all teaching is that it is purposeful, and if the observer has not been told what that purpose is, it's important to be able to discuss it. The same may be said for all the other topics, such as intellectual rigor, a safe and challenging environment, and so on.

> For professional conversations to be nonthreatening, it's essential that all educators have had the opportunity to establish, together, their common expectations about the nature of learning in the school.

With these ideas in mind, then, the informal professional conversations are a consequence of what a supervisor has observed in a classroom and are structured in such a manner to elicit the big ideas through the various topics for conversation. And because the big ideas are complex and are manifested in many different ways, the conversations have the potential to be exceedingly rich. The conversations are journeys, with no correct answers. Even with nontenured teachers, the aim is to explore, together, complex educational issues and to create, together, a way forward in addressing the myriad challenges confronting every teacher. In these conversations, because the issues are complex, the supervisor as well as other teachers who happen to be within earshot, are resources to the process.

Typically, a supervisor will open an informal professional conversation with an observation followed by a question. Particularly if the supervisor was in the classroom for a very short period of time (often less than fifteen minutes) the questions are true questions; the supervisor is not looking for a certain answer. Thus, for example, the supervisor might ask the following:

1. "The (second-grade) students seemed highly engaged in what they were doing with the straws and cylinders. What was the concept they were exploring? What, actually, was their task? It wasn't clear to me, but, of course, I was there for only a few minutes."

2. "I am interested in the worksheet the (fifth-grade) students were completing on the views of different groups prior to the American Revolution about democracy, freedom, laws, and so on. I noticed that the students had very different ideas written down. Did they complete those on their own? Do you plan a general class discussion? What are you planning to do next?"

3. "It seemed to me that while you were facilitating a discussion with one small group of (seventh-grade) students, the other groups were discussing other things (at least the two groups on whom I could eavesdrop were). Is that typical for this class?"

In a school without a well-established professional culture, these questions might appear threatening; indeed, without a consensus that these important matters are always subject to examination, supervisors might be reluctant to ask them. But they reflect important issues. For a supervisor to ignore them is to abdicate an important aspect of one's leadership responsibilities.

It's important to examine what is behind each of the questions.

In the first, the supervisor dropped into a second-grade class and watched while some students were involved in rolling little cylinders down straws that were propped up on books. The students seemed to be enjoying the task; although when asked what they were doing, they did not seem to be sure. The supervisor recognizes that the teacher may have had a very clear purpose in mind and decides to inquire about it. The fact that the students could not explain it does not suggest that the teacher was unclear. The lesson might have been aimed at students' understanding friction, acceleration, or momentum. Whatever it was, the teacher must be clear about purpose and should be able to explain it. So the supervisor asks the teacher to explain her instructional purpose and what the actual task was that the students were doing. Then the conversation can move to how the teacher is advancing student understanding of the concept, what activities and reflection will happen next and so on.

In the second scenario, the observer has walked around the room while the students were comparing notes on their responses to the worksheet. The worksheet itself raised interesting questions related to the perspectives of different groups during the Revolutionary War period. However, the supervisor also noticed that the responses that different students had for different questions were quite different from one another and that, furthermore, some were clearly incorrect. So it's reasonable to inquire about the task, about its intellectual rigor and how student misconceptions would be addressed. This question, like the others, is informed by the topics for conversation and can yield an important exploration of the big ideas.

The third scenario addresses the concept of student engagement in high-level learning and the nature of the tasks they are completing. In this situation, the supervisor has observed that at least some students were not discussing the assigned topic. There are many possible reasons for this, of course. It's possible that they weren't clear about the topic or that (for whatever reason) it did not hold their interest. So a question from a supervisor about patterns of behavior would begin an important conversation about motivation, instructional design, or, perhaps, the challenges presented by particular students.

It's important to note that because the supervisor raises such questions does not suggest deficiency. It's possible, of course, that the ensuing conversations would reveal lack of clarity of purpose (Scenario 1), student confusion (Scenario 2), or lack of student engagement (Scenario 3). But they are just as likely to reveal highly complex thinking on the part of the teacher. Furthermore, the result of such conversations is deepened understanding on the part of the teacher and the supervisor.

Summary

Skill in conducting informal professional conversations is at the heart of educational leadership. And as described in this chapter, these conversations explore the implications of the big ideas (Chapter 3) and reveal the topics for conversation (Chapter 4). When these concepts have been established with a school faculty, within a culture of professional inquiry, the conversations can explore essential issues of teaching and learning. Such explorations and the teacher's reflection on practice they promote are important contributors to ongoing teacher learning.

Informal professional conversations occur within a complex web of relationships and understandings in a school. These cannot be imposed from above or from without; they must be cultivated within the school itself. And because the site administrator is the individual with the greatest positional authority, that individual has an obligation to take the initiative in creating the conditions for productive professional conversations. Issues and procedures to establish those conditions are the focus of the next chapters.

7 Implementation Issues

Professional conversations occur within the cultural context of schools; that culture must support those conversations, enabling them to be honest, substantive, and rewarding. In particular, the conversations must be informed by a shared understanding of the powerful ideas that support high-level learning by students. Thus, before educators in a school can embark on powerful professional conversations and derive the maximum value from them, the conditions must be conducive to such work. So what are the prerequisite conditions for professional conversations, and how do school leaders create those conditions? This chapter describes the many issues involved in putting the ideas in this book into practice. The next chapter outlines some specific actions school leaders might take in that effort.

Finding Time for Conversation

Important conversations about teaching require time; that time must be dedicated and preserved from invasion by competing priorities. Even the preliminary conversations described in this chapter and the next require a commitment of time. This time is an investment in the professional culture of the school; if professional conversations are valued, then the preconditions must be met. And an essential precondition is that all members of the faculty share important concepts about student learning and instructional practice.

It is recommended that school leaders establish, at the beginning of the school year, the schedule for a series of meetings to address the big ideas that undergird daily practice. But before those ideas can be taken up, it's essential to establish that the

> Important conversations about teaching require time; that time must be dedicated and preserved from invasion by competing priorities.

school enjoys a sufficient level of trust to enable those conversations to be honest and candid. These discussions should be scheduled on a regular basis, possibly substituting for some of the time that is normally set aside for faculty or departmental meetings. These conversations (exploring the important ideas described in Chapter 3) may take place in instructional teams, departments, or an entire faculty. The chapter itself can serve as a starting point, with other books and articles taken on as the interest in them is expressed.

Communicating the Purpose

As noted in Chapter 2, "Power and Leadership in Schools," an important use of positional authority in schools is to create a school culture in which everyone in the school—teachers and administrators alike—is engaged in improving student learning. Furthermore, this effort is best achieved not by mandate from the principal's office but through a collegial process in which all educators work through the multiple challenges that comprise everyday practice.

The main vehicle for improving student learning is professional conversation among teachers and between teachers and administrators. These conversations focus on the nature of what students are learning, the design of instructional and assessment tasks to promote that learning and the analysis of student work in response to those activities and assignments. The conversations are generally not a matter of ascertaining whether a teacher is following a certain prescribed methodology. The conversations concern whether students are actually learning what teachers and administrators intend for them to learn, the evidence on which such judgments are made, and the adjustments that must be made to the work in the classroom to ensure that learning is improved.

Indeed, the main purpose of professional conversations is to improve the quality of student learning through collegial dialogue. It's advisable to communicate this purpose explicitly: explaining to the entire faculty that in order to sustain, and indeed improve, learning conditions for students, it's essential that every member of the staff make a commitment to joint effort and improvement of practice. This is a common effort, and it is not being advanced as a corrective or remedial suggestion. Rather, the reason for such an effort is that teaching is extremely complex work, which because it is by definition never perfect, can always be improved. Furthermore, some recent research findings have not yet found their way into the daily practice of many teachers, and it's essential that they do.

> The main vehicle for improving student learning is professional conversation among teachers and between teachers and administrators.

Along with communicating the purpose of professional conversations, it's important to explore the barriers that typically stand in the way of rich professional dialogue. The first concerns the power imbalance between teachers and administrators and the challenge of establishing a level of trust that permits honest conversation. This issue will be addressed more fully below, but at the outset, it's important to recognize, and to encourage others to recognize, its central position at the heart of a professional community.

In addition, part of communicating the purpose of instructional improvement through professional conversations is to establish that there are some big ideas (described in Chapter 3, "The Big Ideas That Shape Professional Conversations") about student learning and about the curriculum design that underlies practice. These big ideas are supported by research but may, in some cases, run counter to popular conceptualizations of how schools operate. For example, many parents of our students think of school as a place where students sit quietly and listen to the teacher. However, while there is a place for teacher presentations in school, few modern educators rely exclusively on lectures to engage students in learning challenging material.

These big ideas give rise to important characteristics of classrooms that serve to structure what an observer sees during a lesson and which serve as the topics for conversation. Such topics are the extent of intellectual rigor and the environment of support and challenge in the classroom. And because of the importance of the big ideas and their implications for practice, such matters are always on the table for conversation. The fact that they are on the table does not suggest, of course, that they are seen to be deficient; rather, they represent the heart of teaching, without which learning does not occur. Therefore, they must serve as the foundation for meaningful conversations about practice.

Recommended procedures for exploring each of these issues (trust, the big ideas, and the topics for conversation) are described below. Specific protocols for dialogue about these matters are offered in the next chapter.

Establishing Trust

Arguably, the most important condition for professional conversations is the existence of trust between teachers and administrators. Without trust, teachers are always on their guard in the presence of their principal, and they tense up whenever an administrator enters their classroom. Discussions during faculty meetings cannot be an honest reflection of professional views if teachers fear retribution or loss of standing if they express a view that is divergent from the official position. In other words, teachers must feel that it is safe to take risks and that they are free to explore issues honestly, without fear that their reputation might be damaged.

It should be noted that an environment of trust among the adults in a school with a safe environment for risk taking, created by the school leader, is analogous to the establishment of

> Arguably, the most important condition for professional conversations is the existence of trust between teachers and administrators.

an environment of respect and rapport by teachers in the classroom. In that context, students must feel that they are safe from ridicule from either their classmates or the teacher if they advance an idea that may be off the mark. They must feel honored and respected by all members of the classroom community. Only then can students learn to their greatest potential.

The first step in establishing an atmosphere of trust in a school is to put it on the table as an issue to be acknowledged and discussed; the administrator should admit publicly that such an atmosphere is a critical precondition to accomplishing other essential work. And if the school has been handicapped in the recent past by a lack of trust between teachers and administrators, the need for such an effort must be discussed openly and suggestions elicited from all members of the faculty as to how that might be achieved and what actions might be undertaken.

Of course, some members of the faculty might be skeptical that an administrator is serious about efforts to improve the atmosphere of trust in the school. A very poor environment, over a number of years, can result in genuine cynicism and alienation; the first agreement that must be reached, then, is a commitment on both sides to address the issue in a serious and honest manner. This cannot be achieved with a single announcement of intent; such a statement may be received with an assumption that it is not authentic, that it is a ploy, or an effort to co-opt teachers. Acknowledging the elephant in the room is tackling the phenomenon of fear and lack of trust that stand in the way of good communication. The elephant, then, must be pulled from underneath the carpet, dragged out in front of everyone and even introduced. "Here it is," we might say, "in the past, many of you have struggled to share concerns openly with the principal. We need to change that culture and I want to hear what you believe will best help us do that."

There are specific actions that school leaders can take, in a number of different areas of the school; these are described briefly below.

Creating a Safe Environment

Many teachers feel profoundly vulnerable in their interactions with administrators. Administrators wield, after all, considerable power within the school, directed primarily through the district's process for teacher evaluation. Thus, a certain level of anxiety on the part of teachers toward administrators is inevitable. Teachers often express concern in sharing their own perceptions of growth areas with their administrator if they feel the school leader will turn around and use the "admission" against them.

But school leaders can, to some extent, defuse the anxiety that teachers feel when an administrator enters their classroom or engages them in conversation. They can do this by, for example,

- establishing with teachers that unless they encounter a serious matter of student safety, they will not use any of the information they collect from informal observations in their evaluations;

- taking no notes during informal observations of teaching; dropping in on classrooms and participating in the learning activities along with the students.

School leaders can defuse the anxiety that teachers feel when an administrator enters their classroom or engages them in conversation.

Acting With Consistency

Teachers find it difficult to fully trust administrators who blow hot and cold in their interactions with them and on their behalf with others, such as parents and central office administrators. Lack of consistency feels, to teachers, as though the rug has been pulled out from under them or that they don't know when the next shoe will drop. It's useful to consider the actions that administrators might take that would serve to undermine teachers' trust in their leadership. A few examples are provided below:

- Despite a commitment to professional consultation with teachers on important matters, an administrator makes an independent decision on a matter of consequence, such as moving to a block schedule.

- An administrator yields to pressure from a parent (perhaps one involved in the parent association) regarding the placement of the parent's child in a class, despite the recommendations of teachers for another placement.

- An administrator conveys an incoherent and inconsistent approach to matters of curriculum and instruction by, for example, advocating for a constructivist program in literacy while promoting a highly prescribed program in mathematics.

- After discussions with faculty, an administrator makes a big push for a certain practice, only to abandon the effort at the first sign of resistance from a small group.

Maintaining Confidentiality

The matter of maintaining confidentiality is not dependent on the disparate power held by teachers and administrators in schools; it is an issue among all individuals regardless of their status in an organization. When we say something in confidence to another person, we have the right to expect that the information will not be shared with others. If we subsequently discover that the others know about it, it serves to undermine (sometimes irremediably) our trust in the other individual; a relationship cannot survive, at least at the same level, that kind of betrayal. Examples of the types of information that might be spread, thus undermining trust, are listed below:

The matter of maintaining confidentiality is an issue among all individuals regardless of their status in an organization.

- Difficulties in one's personal life, such as a pending divorce or a child's struggle with addiction

- A teacher's critical view of a colleague, when the former attempts to maintain a professional relationship

- Critical comments about another school, raising doubts as to whether this person might speak unfavorably of the home school in conversations with educators from other schools

Demonstrating Commitment to Professional Learning

Some administrators convey (even without meaning to) that they are above engaging in the professional development opportunities offered in a school or district. Furthermore, some manage to indicate that they know everything they need to for their responsibilities, and all students would learn at high levels if teachers merely followed the lead of the principal. Such an attitude undermines teachers' trust in their administrators as educators; given the complexity of teaching, teachers can perceive such an attitude as arrogance, while administrators' practice of demonstrating a commitment to continuous learning indicates professional engagement and curiosity.

There are many specific actions school administrators can take to indicate a sincere commitment to their own ongoing professional learning. These actions, together with the explicit expression of the importance of ongoing learning as a mark of all professionals, can go some distance in establishing a culture of professional inquiry in the school. Below are some examples of this:

- Participate along with teachers in inservice offerings. It's important for administrators not to pop in and out but to engage seriously with members of the faculty at a table group and in the activities and discussions of how the approach being presented could be incorporated into the school's own program. Furthermore, when educators engage together in professional activities, they tend to share memorable experiences (some of them amusing) that become part of the shared culture of the school. This shared culture has enormous potential for building and sustaining trust between teachers and principal.

- Describe to teachers a new finding they have recently encountered in the professional literature. This indicates that principals do not consider their own knowledge to be static or that their own days of professional learning are over. If principals invite teachers to comment on the issue, the ensuing conversation reinforces the notion of the entire staff serving as resources to one another, and it conveys an attitude of openness and curiosity on the part of the administrator.

> There are many specific actions school administrators can take to indicate a sincere commitment to their own ongoing professional learning.

Indicating Vulnerability

Teachers may not regard the administrators in their schools as vulnerable in their own profes-sional standing. Particularly if they have been in schools with an authoritarian principal, teach-ers may not recognize that principals are no less vulnerable than they are themselves. Teachers often indicate their favorite part of learning alongside their principal is the time when the school leader shares their own trepidation of applying the new learning in professional development with the faculty ("I am still exploring how best to engage with you in addressing 'problems of practice' that come up in every classroom. I hope we can work on this together.") What follows are some examples of how awareness of vulnerability might be demonstrated:

- Describe, at a faculty or team meeting, an educational puzzlement with which they are struggling. For example, it's not an easy matter to incorporate English language learn-ers into class discussions in, say, a science topic because their vocabulary is severely limited. If teachers have found a way to address this issue, they see their principal as recognizing imperfect understanding and willing to learn from them. Furthermore, the ensuing discussion results in new learning by all teachers because they have the oppor-tunity to share their approaches to a common problem.

- Ask for the advice of faculty members in resolving an issue involving district policy. By describing the issue (for example, district policy regarding a new curriculum) and listening carefully to teachers' comments both in favor and against the pro-posal, the administrator conveys respect for teachers' views and the sense that the school's position on important district issues should reflect the collective wisdom of the school's educators. The administrator, in other words, is not the only expert in these matters.

Once the issue of building trust is suggested for discussion, members of a school faculty, will have many practical ideas for how such trust can be built (and the parallel ways in which it can be undermined). By raising the issue, administrators signal their awareness of its importance and their commitment to building trusting relationships. The conversation often results in a set of norms or operating principles that govern how professional educators behave in their interactions with one another. Such a list might include such things as

- following through on commitments,
- not betraying confidences,
- consulting with colleagues before making significant decisions, and
- participating fully in professional conversations and inservice opportunities.

Develop strategies for both teachers and administrators to convey that a certain action is contrary to their agreed-on principles.

As important as articulating the practical measures that may be taken to build trust is the matter of developing strategies for both teachers and administrators to convey that a certain action is contrary to their agreed-on principles. For example, if a teacher perceives an administrator's attitude regarding a matter before the school as undermining the relationship of trust they have been trying to develop, it's important to be able to bring it up without fear of anger or retribution. This, in itself, requires a high level of trust. Teachers must feel that the environment is safe enough to say to an administrator that they feel, for example, undermined by a decision the principal has made.

School leaders should not expect that trust can be developed quickly or even that by conducting a single discussion of the issue will settle the issue. Trust is a complex matter and, even when painstakingly developed, can be easily undermined. For that reason, it is recommended that school leaders and teachers engage in a series of conversation on the topic, as described in Chapter 8.

Forging Understanding and Consensus on the Big Ideas

In order to have meaningful professional conversations about teaching, teachers and administrators must have shared understanding of the important concepts that underlie their work. Every definition of teaching and every organization of a curriculum rests on certain assumptions regarding how people learn and, indeed, what is worth learning. However, such assumptions are rarely examined explicitly, leading to inconsistencies of practice from one teacher to another and to different expectations between teachers and administrators. This is not to argue for a lockstep approach to instruction: An important outlet for teacher creativity is in the design of techniques to engage students in important learning. Furthermore, teacher sharing of such approaches is an important source of professional dialogue.

But there are important questions that must be addressed because they directly affect the decisions that teachers make on a daily basis. Some examples are listed below.

- Given that preschool children are such keen learners while my class of sixth graders seems so lethargic or even rebellious, what are some strategies I can apply?
- How can I create positive energy in the class?
- I'm noticing a trend in my students to pass notes in class, what are some ways I can focus their attention on their work?
- Why do students become so much more engaged in some activities than in others? How can I increase the amount of student engagement?

- How should I respond when a student offers a poor answer during a class discussion without undermining that student's feelings of self-worth? In fact, how can I ensure that all students participate in discussions instead of them being dominated by just a few?

- Is it important to cover everything in the textbook, even if we have to address lots of it at only a superficial level?

There are many important questions of teaching and learning with which teachers grapple and for which educational research can provide many insights. But the issues are not simple and do not lend themselves to bumper sticker slogans for answers. The questions warrant reading and discussion and may require the use of unfamiliar instructional approaches. The important concepts that underlie teaching and learning have been described briefly in Chapter 3. They have enormous implications for daily practice and, hence, deserve an in-depth exploration by an entire faculty, either as a single group or in instructional teams or departments.

Each of these questions is so important and has such an impact on daily practice that they all deserve careful study and discussion. The outline of a series of meetings on these subjects is provided in Chapter 8. Some of the questions should, of course, be modified according to the specific interests of a group of educators.

What Constitutes Important Learning?

At the present time, many of the traditional assumptions regarding important learning in school are being challenged. Inexorable trends suggest that the ways in which educators and policymakers have organized the curriculum in the past may be inadequate to future demands. In Chapter 3, the rationale behind a forward-looking curriculum was offered, drawing on trends in economics, globalization, and innovation. However, it is possible that a group of educators would find the arguments unconvincing; hence, a serious discussion of the points raised there is warranted. But at the conclusion of the deliberation, educators will be able to develop a set of essential skills and understandings that must be promoted in schools. Below is the list from Chapter 3:

- Deep understanding and skill in the traditional academic disciplines, including written and oral communication

- International understanding

- Innovation, initiative, and creativity

- Critical thinking and problem solving

- Interpersonal skills, including collaboration and leadership

- Knowing how to learn and question

Regardless of the specific items on a list of broad outcomes, the important questions to be explored include the following:

- To what extent does our curriculum reflect these important aspects of learning? If it does not, where can it be strengthened?

- What are the implications for teaching the important learning we have identified? Different instructional skills on the part of teachers are required if we want students to become proficient at, for example, abstract thinking and problem solving as compared to discrete skills that can be simply demonstrated and practiced. Traditional instructional skills will always be needed, but in addition, others will also be required to help students acquire the advanced understanding needed for later success. What are those, and how can teachers attain them?

What Causes Learning?

Research on learning has proceeded over the past century, and our current understanding differs somewhat from that of past generations. Of course, although findings on such a matter could never be considered final, they most assuredly represent an advance over what has been understood previously. Rather than just presenting information and expecting that it will be absorbed, we now know that in order to learn, students must actively process the material. They don't merely *take it in;* they must *understand* it, which requires intellectual activity. In other words, as described in Chapter 3, students must do the following:

- Be mentally active, making connections, formulating hypotheses, and so on

- Link new understanding to what is known

- Participate in in-depth, structured reflection

- Engage in collaboration

Teachers, then, once they have explored the ideas outlined above, may spend productive time, typically in grade-level teams or departments, discussing questions such as the following:

- To what extent do the instructional tasks we use engage students in mental activity?

- How do we draw on what students already know about a topic to help them deepen their understanding?

- What does our analysis of student work tell us about students' level of understanding?

- What opportunities do we provide to students to collaborate with their classmates? When they do collaborate, how can we be sure that all students, not merely a few, are doing the work and attaining understanding?

- To what extent do we enable students to reflect on what they have learned and to develop skills of metacognition?

Many more questions are suggested by the big ideas, presented in Chapter 3, dealing with how students learn; the critical issue is that teachers apply those concepts to their own practice and have the opportunity to learn from their own teaching and that of their colleagues.

How Are Students Motivated?

Understanding what motivates students is of central importance to teachers; every teacher has a compelling mental image of a joyful, purposeful, orderly classroom, in which students are deeply engaged in meaningful work. The reality, however, is frequently somewhat at odds with this image. Students, depending on their own past experiences in school, may be lethargic or even openly rebellious. Furthermore, there are so many of them, and they may be physically larger than the teacher. So how do teachers enlist their enormous energy in active participation?

Chapter 3 reviews the research on motivation and points out the principal human psychological needs, which, if met, contribute to students' active participation in school activities. These are

- belonging and making connections with others,

- competence or mastery,

- autonomy or freedom, and

- intellectual challenge.

Recent research suggests that in order for students to engage deeply with academic material, the classroom activities and assignments should integrate these characteristics. Indeed, activities and assignments may be analyzed with respect to the extent to which they accomplish these things, leading to questions by teachers such as the following:

- How do we organize our classrooms so students have the opportunity to make connections with others? We know that this is important for students and that if we don't build such opportunities into classroom activities, they will find ways to meet this need anyway, perhaps, by passing notes, or texting their friends.

- How do we enable our students to experience the power that comes from mastering complex material? How do we avoid spoon-feeding students what we want them to learn providing them the opportunity to wrestle with understanding?

- To what extent do we provide choice to our students in their work, providing some measure of freedom and autonomy?

- How intellectually challenging are the assignments and activities we use in the classroom and for homework? And given that there is a range of skill and ability in the class, how do we differentiate our assignments so every student is challenged to an appropriate degree?

These questions enable educators to examine what they do in the classroom and the tasks they create for students against the qualities that are shown through recent research to result in heightened energy by students toward learning. The questions may be used, of course, for individual reflection or as the basis of conversation among instructional teams or departments. If used by educators working together, they generate powerful conversation.

What Is Intelligence, and How Do Students' Views Influence Their Actions?

The nature of intelligence and the impact of students' own views of their intelligence on their school performance have been well documented in the research literature. What has emerged from that research is that the prevailing view of intelligence (as fixed and unalterable) in society at large as well as in schools leads to student attitudes of defeatism as soon as they encounter difficulties in their learning. On the other hand, when students are convinced that they become smarter through hard work, they display far more resilience and success in school. Those findings are summarized by the following:

- Students are well served by the acquisition of a malleable view of intelligence.

- Teachers (and parents) can assist in students' development of such a view and of healthy attitudes about their own power in shaping their learning by praising student perseverance and use of strategy in their learning.

Consideration of these matters leads to the discussion of important issues and results in teachers asking themselves questions such as the following:

- How can we encourage students to persevere in difficult tasks even when they don't succeed initially?

- What is the best use of praise for responding to students? How do we prevent the use of praise from actually doing harm to students' sense of their own capabilities?

- Which aspects of students' effort should we emphasize when providing them feedback on their efforts?

These and other questions provide the grist for the mill of important professional conversations among professional educators, whether they are teachers or administrators. They get to the heart of student learning and the interactions between teachers and students.

Elaborating the Topics for Conversation

The topics for conversation described in Chapter 4 are derived directly from the big ideas of Chapter 3 and serve as the foundation of professional conversations within a school. As explained in Chapter 4, these topics are the following:

- Clarity of instructional purpose and accuracy of content
- Safe, respectful, supportive, and challenging learning environment
- Classroom management
- Student intellectual engagement,
- Successful learning by all students
- Professionalism

Many of the ideas embedded in these topics will have been discussed in the conversations of the big ideas; they serve as the practical manifestation of them in the classroom and as the grist for the mill for professional dialogue following an informal classroom visit.

It's important to establish that these topics, at least in their broad outlines, are not a matter for individual discretion. That is, given the implications of the big ideas, every lesson will have clarity of purpose (otherwise, how do teachers know what they intend for students to learn?) and rigorous learning tasks (to ensure mental activity and the development of understanding). Furthermore, every lesson will demonstrate high levels of student energy and engagement (employing the principles of student motivation) and a safe and challenging environment (in which students are challenged to use their minds but in an atmosphere of emotional security). Finally, every class is run as a smooth operation (with students themselves contributing to its functioning) and is engaged in implementing, as appropriate, school and district initiatives.

These topics are always on the table for conversation; however, their actual manifestation will vary considerably from one setting to another. The issue of how they look in practice, following the principles in the big ideas, provides a rich topic for professional discussion. Indeed, following a significant exploration of the big ideas by a school's faculty, it is advised that educators next turn their attention to the topics and discuss them at some detail. If teachers have acquired a solid understanding of the big ideas, the implications of those ideas for practice in the classroom will not be onerous; indeed, they will be recognized as natural implications of those ideas.

Summary

Educators familiar with the framework for teaching will recognize the big ideas as the assumptions that underlie the framework and the topics for conversation as large clusters of the components of the framework. Thus, the ideas in this book complement a school's use of the framework for its foundation of understanding good teaching.

It's essential that all educators in a school understand the big ideas and the topics and accept that they apply to all teaching. This understanding requires time and commitment to acquire high levels of trust among all members of a professional community. But once achieved, educators within a school have the tools for professional conversation available to them.

Suggestions are provided in the following chapter as to how to engage in a series of discussions in school around these ideas, laying the essential groundwork for further professional conversations about daily practice.

8   Conversation Activities for Implementation

As noted in earlier chapters, an appropriate exercise of positional authority in a school is to establish professional consensus on the big ideas that influence learning and therefore teaching. From those big ideas are derived the topics for conversation that are always understood to be worth exploring; school leaders then conduct informal professional conversations as opportunities present themselves. As an extension, it is also an important part of the responsibility of school leaders to equip other individuals in the school—all teachers and both formal and informal teacher leaders—with the background and skills to conduct these same conversations.

But the important questions remain: How does one get started? How do school leaders create the conditions for such professional explorations of practice without creating unnecessary anxiety among the faculty? How can educators undertake important professional conversations in an environment of collegiality, albeit one that recognizes the reality of the power differential among different individuals?

This chapter attempts responses to those important questions with specific tools that may be used as written or (more likely) modified for use. What is envisioned in this chapter is a series of professional conversations in the form of a series of meetings, or within the setting of a book study in which important topics are considered, and faculty have an opportunity to develop a shared understanding. These proposed conversations will, no doubt, be modified by those using them, but they are intended to provide a structure for important dialogue.

The question of the optimal size of a group for such conversations has no single answer; in general, the group should be small enough for everyone to participate and yet sufficiently large for

> It is also an important part of the responsibility of school leaders to equip other individuals in the school—all teachers and both formal and informal teacher leaders—with the background and skills to conduct these same conversations.

a range of views to be represented. Therefore, a group size between five and ten is recommended, although more could be accommodated if care were taken to ensure opportunities for everyone to be involved. This suggests that in a small school, the discussions might include the entire faculty, whereas in a larger school, the meetings would probably be organized within departments or instructional teams.

The study meetings should be facilitated by someone who has developed skills in this important area. If the meetings include the entire school, the natural facilitator is the principal or assistant principal. Alternatively, in a larger school, in which the meetings are conducted within departments or teams, it makes sense for the department chair or team leader to play the facilitative role.

The discussions outlined here are organized around a central question with suggestions as to how teachers might engage with the other teachers, for example, as a large group discussion or individual reflection followed by group sharing at tables. Some indication is also provided of typical responses by teachers with suggestions for possible follow-up questions. But in all cases, the purpose of the discussion is stated clearly, so facilitators, whether they choose to use the recommended prompts or not, have a clear sense of what it is intended for a team of educators to derive from the discussion.

In all cases, if a group develops a keen interest in a topic, it is desirable to undertake additional reading and discussion around that topic. A first source of reading, of course, for the big ideas is Chapter 3 of this book; it is recommended that all teachers have access to that material. Furthermore, Chapter 4 provides an important summary of the topics for conversation. But in addition, in the books and articles cited in the chapters with bibliographic information in the Resources and Suggested Readings section, the various topics are addressed in far greater depth.

Establishing the Foundation

As noted in the previous chapter, time must be set aside not only for professional conversations about teaching but also for establishing the ground rules for those conversations. Honest and candid discussions must be conducted about the need for trust and how to ensure it as well as establishing professional consensus as to the big ideas and the topics for conversation that inform all conversations. It is recommended that school leaders engage in a series of discussions with their faculties—either as a whole or in smaller groups of departments or instructional teams—to establish consensus on these important issues.

These conversations to set the tone deserve careful planning and should be conducted during time set aside for them. Indeed, as will be seen from the discussion below, these conversations could easily consume the better part of an academic year to work through. However, it will be readily appreciated that the time has been well spent.

Communicating the Purpose

The first, essential step in promoting a culture of inquiry, one that permits professional conversations, is to establish the purpose for such conversations. Teachers must have, in other words, a context for the work on which they are about to embark. Explain to the group that it is essential for them to ensure that every student in the school receives a high-quality education and that this is their first priority. The reason for devoting valuable faculty time to the issue is not to suggest that there is something wrong or defective about the quality of teaching currently in place in the school. It is merely to state the obvious: Teaching is enormously complex and can never be perfect. Because it is never perfect, it can always be improved; it is the professional responsibility of each member of the faculty (and oneself as well) to be on a constant quest for improved methods and approaches. Sometimes this requires digging deeply into the thinking that underlies practice and ensuring that everyone in the school holds similar conceptual understanding about the big ideas that help all educators decide what to do on a given day or in a given situation. This is not to suggest that there is a single best way to do things, but there are some important ideas that form the foundation of everything professional educators do in schools; we should not assume that we all understand these or that our understanding could not be strengthened.

> Honest and candid discussions must be conducted about the need for trust and how to ensure it as well as establishing professional consensus as to the big ideas and the topics for conversation that inform all conversations.

Conversation Activity 1:	*Establishing the Contributors to Student Learning*

The Framing Question

Ask teachers to enter into these conversations on the assumption that a shared goal of everyone on the faculty is to promote high-level learning for students. For the moment, ask them to assume that they all know and agree as to what that is. (That question will be addressed in a subsequent session.)

To open the discussion, ask teachers to consider this question: "What are the factors that contribute to student learning?"

Comment on the Question

It's important that teachers don't feel this to be a trick question. If the level of trust is very low based, presumably, on the past culture of the school, it may be difficult to get this discussion going. You may need to offer reassurance that you are not looking

> The first, essential step in promoting a culture of inquiry, one that permits professional conversations, is to establish the purpose for such conversations.

for any particular answer, that there are many correct answers, and that it is important for everyone to share their ideas on this important matter.

Recommended Grouping Pattern

Teachers could, as individuals, consider the question, and you could conduct a general discussion with the entire group. Alternatively, teachers in smaller (e.g., table) groups could address the question, comparing their answers to it. If they work in small groups, one individual should be designated the note taker for the group.

Tools or Prompts

If they begin individually, teachers can write their ideas on a blank piece of paper. Whether teachers initially respond to the question individually or in small groups, you should conduct a general discussion during which you collect their ideas on a board or flip chart. Ask each table group to report one idea from the group's discussion, collapsing similar ideas together, until all ideas have been reported.

As you collect ideas, you should separate them, perhaps using a T-chart, into those over which the school has no control and those over which it does exercise control. For example, the school has no (or very limited) influence over the extent to which students have access to people at home who can help them with their studies. On the other hand, the school (or the school district) has complete control over its curriculum, so long as it addresses the state's content standards. Once the distinction has been made and as new ideas are suggested, elicit from the group where the item should be listed.

Possible Teacher Responses

Depending on the school's situation and the challenges faced by educators, some teachers may focus on factors beyond the influence of the school, a focus that may reflect feelings that improving student performance is beyond their grasp. In fact, it is one of the values of this conversation that teachers are required to recognize that many critical factors important for student learning may be altered by educators, thus setting the stage for enhanced student performance.

The types of ideas that will emerge, that are under the control of the school, are

- the curriculum,
- the quality of teaching,
- the support system for students (Do they have somewhere to get assistance when they encounter difficulty?),

- the master schedule and whether students' experiences are constantly being interrupted, and

- the time available for teacher collaboration and joint planning.

Desired Outcome of the Discussion

It's important for teachers to understand that factors inside and outside the school contribute about equally to student success. But the single most important factor influencing student learning, at least of the factors under the control of the school, is the quality of teaching. And this is a matter for every teacher, working on their own and with colleagues, to be constantly striving to improve.

Conversation Activity 2:	*The Principal's Role in Promoting Good Teaching*

The Framing Question

Next, turn the attention of the group to a related question: "Because we know that the most important factor in student learning (at least within the control of the school) is the quality of teaching, it's essential to understand how it can be improved. Naturally, this is a responsibility for every teacher, but how can an administrator assist in that effort? With respect to the quality of teaching, what is the leader's (principal's or department chair's) responsibility in helping to ensure high quality?"

Comment on the Question

It's not sufficient for school leaders to hire good teachers and hope for the best. Their role must be more proactive than that, working with teachers as fellow educators to engage students in productive learning. As noted in earlier chapters, administrators also have positional authority, which gives them the right—indeed the obligation—to evaluate and help strengthen teacher performance. But for virtually all teachers, their relationship is not one of judge and jury; rather, it is one of colleague.

Recommended Grouping Pattern

This conversation could begin with individual reflection and small group discussion followed by a large group discussion. Alternatively, the discussion could be with the entire group.

Tools or Prompts

No materials are needed for this discussion, although a board or flip chart will be useful to record teachers' thoughts during the large group discussion.

Possible Teacher Responses

In general, teachers will report that they are looking for support from their administrators. It is important to explore what they mean by this. They might be thinking of

- securing instructional materials when teachers need them,
- backing them up in dealing with parents of their students,
- arranging for time for teachers to work together,
- authorization for teachers to attend conferences, or
- assistance in thinking through an instructional situation.

Desired Outcome of the Discussion

This discussion is intended to establish that an important role of administrators is being instructional leaders in the school. They may not have the subject area expertise of teachers, but they can serve as a resource in exploring instructional issues. After all, it is the thesis of this book that an important use of an administrator's positional authority is to engage in informal professional conversations with teachers; it's important for teachers to see the value of those conversations. But if they think of their administrators only as providers of materials and keeper of the master schedule, the potential of such conversations won't be realized.

Establishing Trust

As noted in previous chapters of this book, a leader's ability to influence a school in a positive manner is largely a matter of the level of trust between individuals and in particular between teachers and administrators. This is largely a function, as was pointed out earlier, of the differential amounts of power held by different individuals. When teachers believe themselves to be vulnerable, it can be difficult for them to be completely honest in the presence of an administrator.

There is no simple solution to this difficulty because the power differential is unlikely to be erased; it can't be, given the organization of schools. The best way forward on this matter is to acknowledge, as openly and honestly as possible, the critical importance of high levels of trust in professional relationships and the obligation that everyone has in creating such an environment.

Depending on the situation in a school, this conversation may need to extend over several sessions; teachers may need to come back to an issue that had been discussed previously, to consolidate the shared understandings.

| *Conversation Activity 1:* | *Identifying an Environment of Poor Levels of Trust* |

The Framing Question

To begin the conversation on trust, first mention to the faculty that you are aware of the importance of a high level of trust among everyone and that you are committed to establishing (or improving) it. Acknowledge that this can be a difficult topic for some people and that teachers may not believe, at least initially, that they are able to be completely honest on the matter. Indicate that you want to make every effort to establish a trusting environment in the school and that you will be seeking their advice and feedback on your own behavior and practices.

> Acknowledge, as openly and honestly as possible, the critical importance of high levels of trust in professional relationships and the obligation that everyone has in creating such an environment.

In light of this preliminary explanation, pose the following question to the group: "Have you ever worked in a school in which there were very low levels of trust among people, in particular among teachers and administrators?" Make it clear that you are not asking for them to say things critical of colleagues whom others may know. But if they can tell specific stories with an assurance of anonymity, the conversations will be richer than is possible if the conversations are based on abstractions alone.

After teachers have had an opportunity to share a few ideas, tighten their focus by extending the question in the following manner:

"What contributed to the low level of trust?" and "What were the consequences of the low level of trust?"

Comment on the Question

It is typically easier to describe a negative atmosphere than a positive one, so it has been selected as the starting point for this important conversation. If possible, introduce some levity into the discussion, perhaps offering a reward for the most outrageous action that served to undermine trust in a group.

Recommended Grouping Pattern

This discussion should begin in small groups, perhaps pairs or table groups. It's important for individuals to feel safe and the smaller the group the better. Then conduct a general discussion on the follow-up questions, generating two lists, one corresponding to the answer to "What contributed to the low level of trust?" and "What were its consequences?"

Tools or Prompts

No materials are needed for the first part of the discussion, but a board or flip chart will be required for the second part, the large group discussion.

Possible Teacher Responses

There are many possible responses to this question. For the initial discussion, teachers will have stories to tell, from which the important ideas regarding trust will be extracted. Naturally, the stories themselves will be highly idiosyncratic, and teachers may have to edit them slightly so they do not refer to people known to other teachers.

But when the discussion moves to the extension questions, teachers will cite items such as the following for what contributed to the low level of trust:

- A colleague could not be depended on not to betray a confidence.

- A principal used information that a teacher had shared privately in an evaluation write-up.

- A department chair said she would do something and never followed up.

In the portion of the discussion regarding the consequences of low levels of trust, teachers will contribute items such as the following:

- Teachers decline to be honest with colleagues or administrators.

- Teachers become cynical that anything important will be accomplished; they adopt a this-too-shall-pass attitude, thus ensuring that outcome.

- Teachers adopt a protective attitude toward others and decline to take professional risks.

Desired Outcome of the Discussion

With luck, as a result of this preliminary discussion about trust, members of a school faculty will accept the principal's (or department chair's) sincerity about trying to establish a trusting professional environment and will be willing to engage further with this important topic. However, if the environment in a school has been very negative, it may require a few conversations on the topic before people believe that the leader is committed to a positive environment.

The items listed during the discussion about what contributed to the lack of trust provide the raw material for the next discussion, which will turn to what different individuals can actually do to create or enhance an atmosphere of trust.

Conversation Activity 2:	*Creating and Enhancing a Trusting Environment*

The next conversation derives partly from the previous one about an atmosphere of a lack of trust. However, it too is centered on stories of personal experiences. It will generate ideas for how members of a school faculty can create or enhance an environment of trust in their own setting.

The Framing Question

Introduce this question in a manner similar to the previous one except that this time you are asking people to recall a professional situation in which they experienced high levels of trust. Invite them to share these stories with one another.

Then, as previously, ask teachers to extend their thinking about the question by answering these follow-up questions: "What general characteristics did these environments share?" and "What did you observe that individuals did to create such a trusting environment?"

Comment on the Question

This question does not pose the same difficulties as the previous one in that no one will be even indirectly criticizing another individual who might be known to others in the group. This is a purely positive conversation, intended to generate the characteristics that the faculty would want to emulate as they improve their own culture.

Recommended Grouping Pattern

As in the previous discussion, this question is best answered first by pairs or small groups. Then when you conduct the general discussion, it is best if it includes everyone in the group.

Tools or Prompts

No materials are needed for the initial conversation. However, a board or flip chart will be important for the larger group discussion, in which small groups or pairs share their findings.

Possible Teacher Responses

As in the previous question, there are as many answers to this question as there are individuals to share stories. But the common characteristics extension, teachers will mention such things as the following:

- People were able to be honest with one another; they did not fear reprisals if they took an unpopular position.

- I could approach my principal with a concern without worrying that it would find its way into my evaluation.

For the second extended question, the one relating to what they observed individuals doing to create such an environment, teachers will report such items as the following:

- Administrators listened carefully to teachers and demonstrated respect for their views.

- Everyone in the school could be trusted not to betray a confidence, even when they might have derived some short-term benefit from doing so.

- I could trust that an administrator would follow up on something he said he would do and in a timely fashion.

Desired Outcome of the Discussion

This discussion, together with the previous one, will yield a valuable list of specific characteristics of a healthy and trusting school environment, including specific actions that may be taken (or avoided) by individuals. It will be noted that the responsibility for establishing and maintaining an environment of trust rests primarily with the individual with the greater power—the principal or administrator (or if the position includes supervisory responsibilities, the department chair).

This result is highly significant for framing the next portion of the faculty's exploration of trust and its implications for how they can improve their own culture.

| *Conversation Activity 3:* | *Creating an Action Plan for Trust* |

Following the previous two sessions on the subject of trust, educators (teachers and administrators alike) are in a position to determine how they can, in their setting, improve the trust between teachers and administrators. And because the primary responsibility for establishing a safe and trusting environment must come from the individual with the greater power—namely, the administrator—the bulk of the commitments must come from that side.

The Framing Question

Invite teachers to consider the following question: "Based on what we have concluded over the past few sessions about trust, I'd like you to make some specific suggestions as to what we could do to establish and maintain (or improve) such an environment here."

Comment on the Question

Depending on the history of relationships in the school, the results of this conversation might reflect a significant departure from past practice. Moreover, because there might be individuals present who were responsible (or were perceived to be responsible) for a lack of trust, tact may be needed. And if some teachers believed that the principal was the source of the poor environment (even if that principal is no longer in the school) teachers may be reluctant to be completely honest.

Recommended Grouping Pattern

This conversation should begin with individual reflection followed by sharing in pairs or trios. This will help ensure that the environment is safe, enabling teachers to be as honest as possible. The pairs or trios can then share their thoughts with a few others in a table group and arrive at consensus as to what actions might be taken. Following the small group discussions, it's important to conduct a discussion with the entire group and summarize items on which there is agreement on a board or flip chart.

Tools or Prompts

No materials are needed for this discussion, however, a board or flip chart will be important for the larger group discussion, in which small groups or pairs share their findings.

Possible Teacher Responses

Teachers will have a number of specific suggestions for specific actions that either they or administrators could take that would strengthen the climate in the school and improve the level of trust. They will include such things as the following:

- Conducting frank discussions regarding the level of trust and how it could be improved

- Following through on commitments

- Maintaining confidences

- Participating together in professional development experiences

- Administrators asking teachers for their judgment in professional matters

Desired Outcome of the Discussion

It's important for teachers to recognize that although the burden of establishing a trusting environment rests with the person with greater power, namely, the administrator, teachers play an important role as well. Thus, as items are suggested, for example, following through on commitments, it's important to establish that these same guidelines apply to teachers as well.

An additional issue to be raised concerns the consequences of people violating the agreed-on principles. That is, what should be the response if an individual is found to, for example, have violated a confidence? Is there a sufficient level of trust, in other words, for people to call one another in such a situation? This is a difficult issue, one that may not be comfortable for many teachers to address. One approach is through humor: "What should we do if we find that someone has broken a confidence (or failed to follow through, or some other infraction)? What would be an appropriate punishment? Twenty lashes?" A question such as that will get a little laugh, but it raises a serious matter: How can we, respectfully, point out to a professional colleague that they have let us down in some way?

This is a matter of trust: Do we trust one another enough to be able to be honest, even when it is uncomfortable? This could be discussed at this stage, but probably no commitments will be able to be made. But simply putting the issue on the table is probably sufficient for now.

The Big Ideas: Considering High-Level Learning

Conversations about trust will continue, of course, but it's important for educators to turn their attention now to the big ideas described in Chapter 3, "The Big Ideas That Shape Professional Conversations." These conversations are critical because the big ideas form the foundation of everyday practice in schools.

Stating a commitment to high-level learning is a mantra for both educators and policy makers. But what does it mean? (Simply high scores on state tests?) What does it look like? How would a school's faculty know that it had achieved it? An essential and frequently overlooked aspect of this matter is the central importance of continuing learning for survival in the 21st century. The consideration of high-level learning has several phases; they should be considered in turn.

Conversation Activity 1:	Reflecting on One's Own Recent Learning

The Framing Question

Invite participants to consider what they have learned (what they have had to learn!) since they were twenty-one. These learnings may be from any aspect of their lives: professional or personal.

Comment on the Question

Depending on how old people are, this question might be asking them to consider trends over the past twenty to thirty years. But even with younger people, today's adults have lived through a revolution in information technology, to which they have had to adapt. The aim of this discussion is to encourage reflection on that point and the need for everyone to have highly developed learning-to-learn skills. This conversation makes it personal.

> Stating a commitment to high-level learning is a mantra for both educators and policy makers.

Recommended Grouping Pattern

Because this discussion is not threatening, there is no need to pay particular attention to making the environment safe. Hence, a full group discussion even at the outset could work. On the other hand, if the conversations begin in table groups, everyone is likely to be involved. Then everyone should contribute ideas to a composite list, which may be recorded on a board or flip chart.

Tools or Prompts

Other than a board or flip chart, no materials are needed for this conversation.

Possible Teacher Responses

This conversation may be quite amusing, as teachers recount stories of not being able to make the smartphone work or depending on one's children to help them through the mysteries of social media. They will mention such things as the following:

- Making electronic equipment work, from computers, to smartphones, to PDAs and cameras

- Learning to use a new software program

- Finding their way to a familiar location after the roads have been altered

- Professional learning, such as how to use the writing process or a new inquiry science program

Desired Outcome of the Discussion

Teachers may not have focused their attention on themselves as learners, but this discussion makes it very clear that life in the 21st century requires it. And if it's important for them, it is equally important for their students.

Conversation Activity 2:	**Thinking About the Changing World**

The Framing Question

Ask teachers to contemplate the world of fifty years ago—how have things changed. If possible, show some photographs of the period to spur the imagination. A Google search turns up a number of sites (see the *New York Times*'s American Experience at www.nytstore .com/ProdInter Code.aspx?prodcode=791&intercode=544&minorcode=1432).

Invite teachers to consider different aspects of life in the 50s, such as transportation, communication, the role of and expectations of women, job requirements for different occupations (factory worker, secretary, farmer, and auto mechanic), ethnic composition of the area, beliefs about the environment, and challenges faced by young people.

Comment on the Question

Many of today's students will still be in the workforce fifty years from now. Just as residents of the 1950s could have predicted neither the Internet nor the ubiquitous nature of air travel, it's equally impossible to predict conditions—and therefore specific skills needed—in fifty years.

Of course, many teachers on the faculty will not have been alive in the 1950s, but they will have seen films and will have had conversations with friends and family who lived through that era.

Recommended Grouping Pattern

Small groups would work well for this discussion, with each group focused on one aspect of the changes that have taken place.

Tools or Prompts

A piece of newsprint and markers for each small group enables them to record the results of their discussion, so they can be mounted around the room and discussed. A T-chart format would make the comparisons clear, with one column headed 1950s, and the other headed 2000s.

Possible Teacher Responses

Teachers will comment that many (even most) areas of everyday life have changed profoundly since the 1950s including such things as the following:

- Communications (with smartphones, the Internet, etc.) are vastly more powerful and accessible.

- Many people travel great distances for vacations, although this practice may become more responsive to volatility in fuel prices and people's desire to reduce their carbon footprint.

- Most women are now in the workforce and (while still striving to make equal opportunities a reality) expect at least equal consideration of their qualifications as men.

- All jobs now require extensive familiarity with computer technology. Secretaries used to type and file; they now create databases. Farmers check prices online and adjust their plans according to what they learn. Auto mechanics make use of highly sophisticated computer diagnostic tools. People in these positions have had to learn these skills on the job.

- In virtually all manufacturing plants and many service industries, workers are organized into teams, putting a priority on teamwork and collaboration.

- Most communities have become more ethnically diverse, requiring greater international understanding than was needed in the 1950s.

Desired Outcome of the Discussion

By the conclusion of this discussion, it should be clear to teachers that all workers have now become knowledge workers, our technology has changed irreversibly, the world has really and truly shrunk, and being able to think and reason and to learn new skills are basic for everyone, not just the educationally privileged.

Conversation Activity 3:	**Ensuring Important Learning**

During the previous discussion, someone may have made the observation that the school's curriculum does not always emphasize the types of knowledge and skills that the teachers have been identifying as essential for their students' long-term success. This last discussion addresses two related questions: What is the important learning that we need to ensure for our students, and where in the curriculum can it happen?

The Framing Question

Invite teachers to reflect on the discussions they have participated in during the previous two sessions and to enumerate what knowledge and skill are essential for students to acquire before they graduate.

Ask teachers, once the list of essential learning has been generated, to consider where, every day in their classrooms, students are learning these things.

Comment on the Question

This discussion serves to focus teachers' attention on the meaning of the term *high-level learning*: It implies thinking and reasoning, environmental and cultural sensitivity, and so on. And although some schools, at the middle and high school levels, may offer courses in global issues or environmental studies, relatively few students will have access to them. And the cognitive and collaborative skills must be incorporated into every discipline.

Recommended Grouping Pattern

This discussion is best conducted with the full group because a number of similar ideas will be voiced, and they can be combined.

> By the conclusion of this discussion, it should be clear to teachers that all workers have now become knowledge workers, our technology has changed irreversibly, the world has really and truly shrunk, and being able to think and reason and to learn new skills are basic for everyone, not just the educationally privileged.

Tools or Prompts

The T-charts produced during the previous session would be valuable here; as teachers review what they produced as to how the world is changing, they will be reminded of the types of learning outcomes they must ensure for their own students.

Possible Teacher Responses

The first question will generate a number of ideas similar to those described in Chapter 3, although these should not be considered to be the only right answers to the question. And depending on what material teachers have been reading, their thoughts may diverge somewhat from these ideas. However, it is hoped that most of the ideas below will be incorporated into the discussion:

- Deep understanding and skill in the traditional academic disciplines
- International understanding
- Innovation and creativity
- Abstract thinking and problem solving
- Interpersonal skills
- Knowing how to learn new things

The second question will produce thoughtful comments as to the difficulty of incorporating even critically important concepts and skills into an already-full curriculum. These concerns will probably be offset, however, by the recognition that not incorporating such things into the school day of every student is really not an option.

Desired Outcome of the Discussion

Through skilled facilitation, most teachers will recognize that the important knowledge and skills their students must acquire are not an add-on to their busy days. Rather, things such as thinking, interpersonal skills, and learning-to-learn skills may be incorporated into virtually any discipline.

Prior to the next session, ask teachers to prepare for the discussion by spending about thirty minutes watching a young child at work or play. They could use their own children for this assignment or other young children they know. Or if they don't have easy access to young children, they could go to a local playground and observe some children there.

How Do People Learn?

This segment of the discussions among teachers are, arguably, the most important of the entire sequence, because they get into the specifics of what teachers do every day as they plan for student learning and execute their plans. It's one thing to be clear about what we want students to learn, but how do they learn it? As with many aspects of schools, it turns out that the conventional wisdom is not borne out by the research into the matter. It is not even borne out by teachers' own personal experiences with both children and adults. As with some of the other topics, several sessions are devoted to this topic.

| *Conversation Activity 1:* | *Summarizing Observations From Personal Experience* |

Teachers have ample opportunity to discern, from their everyday experience, the essential characteristics of human learning. Every parent has experienced the unrelenting energy of small children making sense of their environment by exploring the closets in the home, climbing on structures, and otherwise endangering themselves or others. They tirelessly ask, "Why?" prompting their elders to finally announce that it is "Just the way it is!" Older children are more sophisticated in their explorations but are similarly indefatigable. This discussion is intended to highlight the nature of learning in young children and how that contrasts with what they may observe with older students.

The Framing Question

"What did you notice about the child you were observing including his or her actions, ways of solving problems (such as climbing over something), energy level, and so on? How does this contrast, if at all, with what you observe with older children, either at home or in school?"

Comment on the Question

This question enables teachers to draw on their experiences with young children outside the school setting and lays the groundwork for additional conversations about designing learning experiences for students. What often emerges from these discussions is that young children have tremendous energy for learning new things and that some of this energy dissipates by the time they have been in school for very long.

Recommended Grouping Pattern

This question is best considered, first of all, in small groups where teachers can share their observations and derive the general principles from all the different stories that are shared. The small group discussions should be followed by a full group conversation in which the characteristics of the learners are shared.

It's one thing to be clear about what we want students to learn, but how do they learn it?

Tools or Prompts

It's helpful for this discussion for teachers to have a place to record their collective observations, such as the chart in Figure 8.1.

Figure 8.1 Collective Conversation Recording Device

Young Children	Adolescents
Observations	
Characteristics of the Learners	

Possible Teacher Responses

Teachers will almost certainly note the following characteristics of young children in their learning:

- Young children have tremendous energy for learning. In fact, this energy is often exhausting to their parents or other caregivers.

- Young children are extremely curious about their environment and explore it endlessly, not even wanting to stop for sleep.

- Older children, when doing things that intrigue and challenge them (such as playing video games or learning to ride a skateboard) have tremendous energy for the task. But when asked to do something they don't want to do, they may demonstrate real lethargy.

Desired Outcome of the Discussion

With luck and skilled facilitation, teachers will recognize from their own experience and this conversation that children have enormous energy for learning; part of our challenge as teachers is to capture that energy and enlist it for school tasks.

Conversation Activity 2:	*Reflecting on One's Own Learning*

Another important insight into learning may be derived from considering one's own approach to learning; this conversation, combined with the earlier discussion about children and their learning, can yield powerful insights into considerations about planning for student engagement.

The Framing Question

"Consider for a moment how you learn. Think of something that you have learned—something important. How did this happen? This could be in an academic setting or in another setting. But think about your learning and describe the situation briefly to others at your table."

Comment on the Question

This conversation again enables teachers to extract important pedagogical principles from their own experiences. When asked to consider their own learning, teachers must remove themselves from their supposed professional knowledge and reflect on experience; this can be done—indeed, *must* be done—removed from educational jargon and pseudoknowledge.

Recommended Grouping Pattern

This conversation should be conducted first in table groups and then in a large group. The focus of the large group discussion should be on the patterns about learning that teachers detected from their stories and whether there are general rules that could be concluded.

Tools or Prompts

The results of the large group discussion should be collected on a flip chart.

Possible Teacher Responses

In general, teachers will probably conclude that their greatest learning occurred when they were actively engaged mentally in a task, perhaps even physically active (depending on what it was that was being learned). Teachers rarely recall important learning from listening to a lecture or reading a textbook.

Desired Outcome of the Discussion

The aim of this discussion is for teachers to realize that for themselves, learning depends on their own active involvement. Learning by students is similar; it is not something done *to* students; rather, it depends on what students themselves *do*.

Worthwhile Learning Experiences

Through watching children at play and work and through analyzing their own experiences in learning, teachers can determine important characteristics of learning experiences. They can also derive them from their experiences of teaching. This discussion is intended to elicit these characteristics.

Conversation Activity 1:	***Reflecting on the Characteristics of Children's Learning***

The Framing Question

"Think about your experiences in teaching and recall a particularly successful lesson, one in which your students were highly engaged and from which they learned a lot. Briefly describe this lesson to others at your table."

Comment on the Question

Some clarification of this question may be needed in that some teachers might relate an activity that students found fun but one from which they did not learn very much. Alternatively, some teachers might think of an activity in which students were busy but not intellectually engaged. That is, they might have been on task in the sense of completing an assignment. But if the assignment itself was unchallenging or did not constitute high-level learning, then it would not contribute to student engagement.

Recommended Grouping Pattern

This conversation should begin in small groups, with teachers telling their stories to one another. After they have recalled their stories, teachers should be encouraged to discern common patterns from different stories and identify the characteristics, in general, of engaging activities and assignments. Then conduct a general discussion with the entire group and create a list of agreed on characteristics of engaging learning activities.

Tools or Prompts

A flip chart will be needed to collect comments from the different table groups.

Possible Teacher Responses

Teachers will identify a number of characteristics of engaging learning experiences including some or all of the following:

- Pose an interesting problem or question

- Invite student choice and initiative

- Encourage depth rather than breadth

- Permit collaborative work

- Require higher-level thinking (e.g., collecting and analyzing information or making predictions)

Desired Outcome of the Discussion

It's important for teachers to recognize the critical point of these discussions: that intellectual engagement is essential for student learning. In essence, learning is done *by the learner,* through active intellectual engagement. Put another way, we are tempted, as teachers, to think that our students learn on account of what we do. That would be a mistake; our students don't learn because of what *we* do; they learn because of what *they* do. Our challenge then, as teachers, is to design learning experiences for students that are intrinsically interesting and that will yield the learning we want.

Human Motivation

High levels of student learning require commitment on the part of students. It's not sufficient for teachers and parents to want students to learn well; students, particularly in middle and high school years, must work to acquire complex concepts and skills. But what motivates them to exert such effort, apply such mental elbow grease? Is it only the rewards of high grades (or with younger children, tokens such as gold stars)? What is the difference between extrinsic and intrinsic motivation, and how can teachers help student develop the latter?

> Our students don't learn because of what *we* do; they learn because of what *they* do.

What is the difference between extrinsic and intrinsic motivation, and how can teachers help student develop the latter?

Provide a summary of the research on motivation conducted by William Glasser (1986) and Edward Deci (1995) among many others. Point out that all human beings share some important psychological needs: These are (as indicated in Chapter 3) listed below:

- *Belonging and making connections with others.* Human beings are social creatures and must make connections with others. Both adults and children are more motivated to participate in an activity in which they can engage with others.

- *Competence or mastery.* All people derive enormous satisfaction from achieving something difficult. Part of the satisfaction is the struggle itself; if it's too easy, if there is no challenge, the result is cheapened.

- *Autonomy or freedom.* No one likes being told what to do; this is well known to parents who might ask their three-year-old whether they would like to get ready for bed now or in five minutes?

- *Intellectual challenge.* Everyone enjoys a challenge, both adults and children. This helps explain the appeal of crossword puzzles and Sudoku.

Point out that these are essential, fundamental needs shared by all humans, adults and children alike. Mention that they will spend a few sessions exploring these ideas and their implications for how we organize learning experiences in school.

Conversation Activity 1:	*Considering Adult Motivation*

As with other parts of these conversations, it is helpful for teachers to derive important principles from their own experiences. Therefore, the conversation about motivation will begin with how teachers' own needs, as identified by Glasser (1986) and Deci (1995) among others, are met. The conversation will focus on teachers' professional experiences because school life is shared by them all.

The Framing Question

"Think about your life in school and the school as an organization. How are teachers' needs for connecting, competence, freedom, and intellectual challenge met? Can you think of ways we could improve how we meet these needs?"

Comment on the Question

This question is straightforward and should need little or no clarification. It may be an unfamiliar concept, however, because most teachers think of their schools as places where students' needs are considered but teachers' needs are not. Therefore, they may be surprised to discover that schools or organizations can be structured in ways to make them more rewarding for the adults who spend many of their waking hours there.

Recommended Grouping Pattern

This conversation can begin in small groups with, perhaps, a need assigned to each group. The groups can consider the need assigned to them and then report out during a full group discussion.

Tools or Prompts

None are absolutely needed, but a worksheet similar to the one in Figure 8.2 (see next page) might be helpful.

Possible Teacher Responses

This conversation helps teachers recognize that although schools can be satisfying places to work, they can usually be improved for the adults in them. They may report such things as the following:

- Being part of an instructional team helps me feel connected with others, but if we were able to meet more regularly, it would be improved.

- Our staff parties are important to me.

- Helping a struggling student finally succeed is very satisfying to me and makes me feel competent and capable.

- The directives we get from central office undermine my feelings of autonomy; is there anything we can do about that?

- Figuring out how to present this concept is really challenging, but I enjoy the struggle.

Desired Outcome of the Discussion

Considering the issue of psychological needs from their own perspective helps make the concept real to teachers. It can also provide ideas for them to work on improving the school not only in terms of its results with students but as a place for adults to work.

Conversation Activity 2:	*Considering Student Motivation*

Once teachers have applied the theories of motivation to their own experience, they can turn their attention to their students and consider how those ideas can and should affect their practice.

Figure 8.2 Meeting Our Needs

1. Circle the need assigned to your group here:

Belonging   Competence   Autonomy   Challenge

2. Note some specific examples of how this fundamental need, for teachers, is met in our
   school.

_____

_____

_____

_____

_____

_____

_____

_____

3. Also generate some suggestions for how our school could further address this need.

_____

_____

_____

_____

_____

_____

_____

_____

_____

_____

The Framing Question

"What opportunities do our students have to satisfy their needs for connecting with others both through what they experience in the classroom and through other programs in which they participate?"

Comment on the Question

Most teachers think in terms of *teaching* their students, not in terms of their students' needs as human beings. However, this discussion is likely to help teachers recognize that when they do incorporate these considerations both in how they teach and in their design of student programs, students are far more engaged in learning.

Recommended Grouping Pattern

This conversation is best conducted in small groups, with teachers clustered by grade levels or departments. The small groups should be asked to provide a brief summary of their conclusions to the full group.

Tools or Prompts

None are absolutely needed, but a worksheet similar to the one in Figure 8.3 (see next page) might be helpful.

Possible Teacher Responses

Teachers will report such things as the following:

- I can see now why group work is so important in my teaching.

- The other day one of my students was so elated when he finally understood how to factor polynomials! He felt so *powerful!*

- I should try to offer students more choices in what I ask them to do, and I need to make sure that whichever choice they make will result in high-quality learning.

- I wonder whether we could incorporate more puzzlements into our science lessons.

Desired Outcome of the Discussion

This conversation should highlight the fact that often rather small adjustments in practice can make a big difference in terms of student commitment to and involvement in learning. The theories regarding psychological needs are very helpful for teachers in knowing which adjustments to make. Teachers should recognize that these theories also provide a stronger rationale for the design of learning experiences, which they discussed in the previous segment. These should be reviewed now and considered in light of the theory of motivation in

Figure 8.3 Meeting Student Needs

Generate examples of how our school is, or could be, satisfying each of the psychological needs identified by William Glasser (1986) and Edward Deci (1995).

Belonging

_____

_____

_____

_____

Competence

_____

_____

_____

_____

Autonomy

_____

_____

_____

_____

Challenge

_____

_____

_____

_____

addition to that of learning. That conversation pointed out that good instructional activities are ones that

Often rather small adjustments in practice can make a big difference in terms of student commitment to and involvement in learning.

- pose an interesting problem or question,

- invite student choice and initiative,

- encourage depth rather than breadth,

- permit collaborative work, and

- require higher-level thinking (e.g., collecting and analyzing information or making predictions).

Topics for Conversation

It is now time to bring the process to consideration of the essential aspects of practice that should always be available for professional conversation. It was stated earlier in this book that an important use of a principal's positional authority is to forge common understanding of critical concepts and to explore the application of these concepts in the school. The big ideas are those critical concepts, and they have been explored in some depth. Teachers can now delve into their application to classroom practice.

As stated in Chapter 4, the topics always available for rich professional conversation are the following:

- Clarity of instructional purpose and accuracy of content

- Safe, respectful, supportive and challenging learning environment

- Classroom management

- Student intellectual engagement

- Successful learning of all students

- Professionalism

Discussion Questions 1 Through 6: Considering the Topics for Conversation

Point out to teachers that as you walk around the school and drop into classrooms, you want to be able to engage in meaningful professional conversations with them. Moreover, you hope that the conversations they have with one another are rich and productive. Review the items above, indicating that these topics are derived directly from the big ideas and that it's important for everyone in the school to be able to discuss them. You may also have to point out that discussing them does not suggest that you believe that classroom practice is deficient. Far from it! But teaching is extremely challenging work and can always be strengthened. The conversations are for the purpose of ongoing and continuous improvement, part of the mission of every professional educator.

The Framing Question

"What would one see or hear, from either the students or the teacher, in a classroom in which teachers were able to implement these ideas at a high level? Can you think of some specific examples? Furthermore, how would such teachers talk about their work?"

Comment on the Question

These conversations permit teachers to try out their ideas in a safe environment, with their colleagues, without the sense that their administrator is listening for a specific response. In fact, it's important to emphasize that there are no correct answers to the questions and that they are designed to promote reflection and conversation.

Recommended Grouping Pattern

Small groups, probably grade-level or departmental groups, are best for the conversation. It is recommended that six sessions be devoted to discussions on this subject, with one topic addressed at each session. If small groups note their ideas on a piece of newsprint, these charts can then be used either as material for a gallery walk or as the basis for a report out by each group, followed by a large group discussion of the topic.

If the school is using the framework for teaching, the links between these topics and the components of the framework can constitute another important conversation. A guide to this link is provided in Chapter 4.

Tools or Prompts

No tools other than newsprint are needed for this discussion.

Possible Teacher Responses

Teacher responses will vary enormously, of course, but may include such things as the following:

- For clarity of instructional purpose and accuracy of content
  - A teacher, in conversation following a lesson, states very clearly what she intended for the students to learn.
  - The activities and materials are suitable to the teacher's purpose.

- For a safe, respectful, supportive and challenging learning environment
  - Students are never observed being ridiculed or put down either by the teacher or by their classmates.
  - The teacher refuses to accept sloppy, inadequate work from students.
  - Students are praised for their effort and the strategies they use in their work.

- For classroom management
  - There is very little loss of time due to noninstructional matters.
  - Students themselves see to it that the class runs smoothly.
  - The teacher is required to make only occasional comments to students about their behavior.

- For student intellectual engagement
  - Students are required to think, analytically or creatively.
  - Assignments and activities are designed to have multiple correct answers or many approaches to a single answer.
  - Students are engaged in vibrant discussions regarding their work.
  - There is a level of buzz in the classroom; students know what they are to do, and they get on with it with a minimum of teacher direction.
  - Every student is engaged in the activities.

- For successful learning of all students
  - The teacher monitors student understanding during the lesson.
  - The teacher has created questions or approaches (such as exit tickets) to determine each student's success on the outcomes of the lesson.
  - The teacher adjusts a lesson or locates supplemental resources to assist students who are experiencing difficulty.
  - Students themselves assess their own work.

- For professionalism
  - Teachers engage in professional learning activities, either on their own or with colleagues.
  - Teachers' record-keeping is accurate, and (for instructional matters) can be used for planning.
  - Teachers communicate with the families of their students frequently, both about the instructional program and about the progress of individual students.
  - Teachers participate in school and district professional activities.

Desired Outcome of the Discussions

Teachers should emerge from these conversations with a sense of the broad range of possible approaches to the different topics under discussion. They will develop confidence that their ideas are good ones and will also express appreciation for the ideas of their colleagues. It is hoped that this entire series of conversations will serve to defuse teachers' apprehensions about being involved in professional conversations with their principals and that they will be able to embark on them with the expectation of rewarding encounters.

Summary

Most schools have not, historically, been organized to engage teachers in rich professional conversations, particularly not with their principals or other supervisors. However, after engaging in a series of discussions, as outlined in this chapter, a school faculty should have acquired important shared understanding of essential big ideas that underlie practice and a sense of how these are manifested in the classroom. Furthermore, because of the first discussions, these conversations will be able to be conducted within an environment of trust.

References and Suggested Readings

Arneson, S. M. (2014). *Building trust in teacher evaluations: It's not what you say; it's how you say it.* Thousand Oaks, CA: Corwin.

Barnard, C. I. (1958). *The functions of the executive.* Cambridge, MA: Harvard University Press.

Barrell, J. (1991). *Teaching for thoughtfulness: Classroom strategies to enhance intellectual growth.* White Plains, NY: Longman.

Barrell, J. (2003). *Developing more curious minds.* Alexandria, VA: ASCD.

Bennis, W. (2003). *On becoming a leader* (3rd ed.). Cambridge, MA: Basic Books.

Binet, A. (1975). *Modern ideas about children* (S. Heisler, Trans.). Menlo Park, CA: Suzanne Heisler.

Black, P., Harrison, C., Lee, C., Marshall, B., & Wiliam, D. (2003). *Assessment for learning: Putting it into practice.* Philadelphia, PA: Open University Press.

Bosk, C. L. (1979). *Forgive and remember: Managing medical failure.* Chicago, IL: University of Chicago Press.

Boyer, E. (1983). *High school: A report on secondary education in America.* New York, NY: Harper & Row.

Brounstein, M. (2000). *Coaching and mentoring for dummies.* New York, NY: Wiley.

Coleman, J. (1966). *Equality of educational opportunity.* Washington, DC: National Center for Educational Statistics.

Collins, J. (2001). *Good to great: Why some companies make the leap and others don't.* New York, NY: HarperCollins.

Common Core State Standards. (2015). Retrieved from http://www.corestandards.org/

Costa, A. L., & Garmston, R. J. (2002). *Cognitive coaching: A foundation for renaissance schools* (2nd ed.). Norwood, MA: Christopher Gordon.

DeGrasse, L. (2001, January 11). Excerpts from judge's ruling on school financing. *New York Times.* Retrieved from http://www.nytimes.com/2001/01/11/nyregion/excerpts-from-judge-s-ruling-on-school-financing.html

Danielson, C. (2007). *Enhancing professional practice: A framework for teaching.* Alexandria, VA: ASCD.

Deci, E. (1995). *Why we do what we do: Understanding self-motivation.* New York, NY: Putnam.

Dewey, J. (1959). *Dewey on education: Selections.* New York, NY: Teachers College Press.

Dweck, C. S. (2000). *Self-Theories: Their role in motivation, personality, and development.* Philadelphia, PA: Psychology Press.

Dweck, C. S. (2006). *Mindset: The new psychology of success.* New York, NY: Random House.

Dweck, C. S. (2014, December). Teachers' mindsets: "Every student has something to teach me." *Educational Horizons, 93*(2), 10–14.

Feiner, M. (2004). *The Feiner points of leadership: The 50 basic laws that will make people want to perform better for you.* New York, NY: Warner Business Books.

Fogarty, R. (Ed.). (1998). *Problem based learning: A collection of articles.* Arlington Heights, IL: Skylight.

Fosnot, C. T. (1989). *Enquiring teachers, enquiring learners: A constructivist approach to teaching*. New York, NY: Teachers College Press.

Friedman, T. L. (2007, June 10). Israel discovers oil. *New York Times*. Retrieved from http://select.nytimes.com/2007/06/10/opinion/10friedman.html?_r=1&oref=slogin

Fullan, M. (2005). *Leadership and sustainability: Systems thinkers in action*. Thousand Oaks, CA: Corwin.

Gallagher, S. A., & Stepien, W. J. (1996). Content acquisition in problem-based learning: Depth versus breadth in American studies. *Journal for the Education of the Gifted, 19*(3), 257–275.

Ginnott, H. G. (1969). *Between parent and teenager*. New York, NY: Macmillan.

Glasser, W. (1986). *Control theory in the classroom*. New York, NY: Perennial Library.

Glasser, W. (2001). *Every student can succeed*. Chula Vista, CA: Black Forest Press.

Glickman, C. D., Gordon, S. P., & Ross-Gordon, J. M. (2003). *SuperVision and instructional leadership: A developmental approach* (6th ed.). Boston, MA: Allyn & Bacon.

Goleman, D. (1995). *Emotional intelligence*. New York, NY: Bantam.

Goodlad, J. I. (1984). *A place called school: Prospects for the future*. New York, NY: McGraw-Hill.

Greene, D., & Lepper, M. (1974). How to turn play into work. *Psychology Today, 8*(4), 49–52.

Herzberg, F., Mausner, B., & Snyderman, B. (1993). *The motivation to work*. New Brunswick, NJ: Transaction.

Hiebert, J., Carpenter, T. P., Fennema, E., Fuson, K. C., Murray, H., & Wearne, D. (1997). *Making sense: Teaching and learning mathematics with understanding*. Portsmouth, NH: Heinemann.

Hiebert, J., Stigler, J. W., Jacobs, J. K., Givvin, K. B., Garnier, H., Smith, M., . . . Gallimore, R. (2005). Mathematics teaching in the United States today (and tomorrow): Results from the TIMSS 1999 video study. *Educational Evaluation and Policy Analysis, 27*(2), 111–132.

Holliday, M. (2001). *Coaching, mentoring, and managing* (2nd ed.). Franklin Lakes, NJ: Career Press.

Jackson, D. B. (2003, April). Education reform as if student agency mattered: Academic microcultures and student identity. *Phi Delta Kappan, 84*, 579–591.

James, W. (1983). *Talks to teachers on psychology: And to students on some of life's ideals*. Cambridge, MA: Harvard University Press.

Johnson, S. M. (1990). *Teachers at work: Achieving success in our schools*. New York, NY: Basic Books.

Jung-Beeman, M., Bowden, E. M., Haberman, J., Frymiare, J. L., Arambel-Liu, S., Greenblatt, R., . . . & Kounios, J. (2004). Neural activity when people solve verbal problems with insight. *Public Library of Science Biology, 2*(4).

Kelly, R. E. (1998). In praise of followers. *Harvard Business Review, 88*(6), 142–148.

Kohn, A. (1993). *Punished by rewards: The trouble with gold stars, incentive plans, A's, praise and other bribes*. Boston, MA: Houghton Mifflin.

Kramer, R. M. (1996). Divergent realities and convergent disappointments in the hierarchic relation: Trust and the intuitive auditor at work. In R. M. Kramer & T. R. Tyler (Eds.), *Trust in organizations: Frontiers of theory and research* (pp. 216–245). Thousand Oaks, CA: Sage.

Lipton, L., & Wellman, B. M. (2000). *Pathways to understanding: Patterns and practices in the learning-focused classroom* (2nd ed.). Sherman, CT: Mira Via.

McPhee, J. (1966). *The headmaster: Frank L. Boyden of Deerfield*. New York, NY: Farrar, Straus & Giroux.

Mishra, A. K. (1996). Organizational responses to crisis: The centrality of trust. In R. M. Kramer & T. R. Tyler (Eds.), *Trust in organizations: Frontiers of theory and research* (pp. 261–287). Thousand Oaks, CA: Sage.

National Research Council. (1999). *How people learn: Bridging research and practice*. Washington, DC: National Academies Press.

Nigro, N. (2003). *The everything coaching and mentoring book: How to increase productivity, foster talent, and encourage success*. Avon, MA: Adams Media.

Perkins, D. N. (1992). *Smart schools: From training memories to educating minds*. New York, NY: Free Press.

Peters, T., & Austin, N. (1985). *A passion for excellence: The leadership difference*. New York: Random House.

Reina, D. S., & Reina, M. L. (2006). *Trust and betrayal in the workplace: Building effective relationships in your organization* (2nd ed.). San Francisco, CA: Berrett-Kohler.

Resnick, L. B., & Klopfer, L. E. (Eds.). (1989). *Toward the thinking curriculum: Current cognitive research*. Alexandria, VA: ASCD.

Rock, D. (2006). *Quiet leadership: Six steps to transforming performance at work*. New York, NY: HarperCollins.

Sarason, S. B. (1991). *The predictable failure of educational reform: Can we change course before it's too late*. San Francisco, CA: Jossey-Bass.

Senge, P. M. (1990). *The fifth discipline: The art and practice of the learning organization*. New York, NY: Doubleday.

Senge, P. M., Cambron-McCabe, N., Lucas, T., Smith, B., Dutton, J., & Kleiner, A. (2000). *Schools that learn: A fifth discipline fieldbook for educators, parents, and everyone who cares about education*. New York, NY: Doubleday.

Sergiovanni, T. J. (1992). *Moral leadership: Getting to the heart of school improvement*. San Francisco, CA: Jossey-Bass.

Shulman, L. S. (2004). *The wisdom of practice: Essays on teaching, learning, and learning to teach*. San Francisco, CA: Jossey-Bass.

Silverman, L., & Taliento, L. (2005). *What you don't know about managing nonprofits—and why it matters*. New York, NY: McKinsey & Company.

Stigler, J. W., & Hiebert, J. (1999). *The teaching gap: Best ideas from the world's teachers for improving education in the classroom*. New York, NY: Free Press.

Taba, H., & Elzey, F. (1964). Teaching strategies and thought processes. *Teachers College Record, 65*, 524–534.

Tschannen-Moran, M. (2004). *Trust matters: Leadership for successful schools*. San Francisco, CA: Jossey-Bass.

Tschannen-Moran, M., & Hoy, W. K. (1998). A conceptual and empirical analysis of trust in schools. *Journal of Educational Administration, 36*, 334–352.

Visscher, M. (2006). Reading, writing, and playing "The Sims": What video games can teach educators about improving our schools. *Ode, 4*(7), 18–23.

von Glasersfeld, E. (1989). Cognition, construction of knowledge, and teaching. *Synthese, 80*, 121–140.

Whitaker, T., Whitaker, B., & Lumpa, D. (2000). *Motivating and inspiring teachers: The educational leader's guide for building staff morale*. Larchmont, NY: Eye on Education.

White, R. W. (1959). Motivation reconsidered: The concept of competence. *Psychological Review, 66*, 297–333.

Whitmore, J. (2002). *Coaching for performance: GROWing human potential and purpose* (3rd ed.). Boston, MA: Nicholas Brealey.

Index

A SAGE Company

Helping educators make the greatest impact

CORWIN HAS ONE MISSION: to enhance education through intentional professional learning.

We build long-term relationships with our authors, educators, clients, and associations who partner with us to develop and continuously improve the best evidence-based practices that establish and support lifelong learning.

Solutions you want. Experts you trust.
Results you need.

AUTHOR CONSULTING

Author Consulting

On-site professional learning with sustainable results! Let us help you design a professional learning plan to meet the unique needs of your school or district. www.corwin.com/pd

INSTITUTES

Institutes

Corwin Institutes provide collaborative learning experiences that equip your team with tools and action plans ready for immediate implementation. www.corwin.com/institutes

ECOURSES

eCourses

Practical, flexible online professional learning designed to let you go at your own pace. www.corwin.com/ecourses

READ2EARN

Read2Earn

Did you know you can earn graduate credit for reading this book? Find out how: www.corwin.com/read2earn